JACKIE KENDALL & DEBBY JONES

THE RIGHT GUY FOR THE RIGHT GIRL

BECOMING THE MAN OF HER DREAMS

Destiny Image® Publishers, Inc.
P.O. Box 310
Shippensburg, PA 17257-0310

*"Speaking to the Purposes of God for This Generation
and for the Generations to Come."*

Formerly published as
Lady In Waiting Second Edition © 1995 ISBN 1-56043-848-7
Lady in Waiting Meditations For the Heart © 2002 ISBN 0-7684-3034-8
Lady In Waiting Study Guide © 2002 ISBN 1-56043-298-5
Lady in Waiting Expanded Edition © 2005 ISBN 0-7684-2310-4

Trade Paper ISBN 978-0-7684-3256-5
Hardcover ISBN 978-0-7684-3454-5
Large Print ISBN 978-0-7684-3455-2
Ebook ISBN 978-0-7684-9112-8

For Worldwide Distribution
Printed in the U.S.A.
1 2 3 4 5 6 7 8 9 10 / 16 15 14 13 12 11 10

This book and all other Destiny Image, Revival Press, MercyPlace, Fresh Bread, Destiny Image Fiction, and Treasure House books are available at Christian bookstores and distributors worldwide.

For a U.S. bookstore nearest you, call 1-800-722-6774.
For more information on foreign distributors, call 717-532-3040.
Or reach us on the Internet: www.destinyimage.com.

CONTENTS

Preface 5

Chapter 1 Man of Reckless Abandonment . . 9

Chapter 2 Man of Diligence 29

Chapter 3 Man of Faith 51

Chapter 4 Man of Virtue 69

Chapter 5 Man of Devotion 89

Chapter 6 Man of Purity 109

Chapter 7 Man of Security 137

Chapter 8 Man of Contentment 155

Chapter 9 Man of Conviction 175

Chapter 10 Man of Patience 201

PREFACE

Is this just another book for singles? No! We believe this book is unique because its emphasis is not on a man's status (single, married, divorced, or widowed), but on the state of his heart. We want to direct a man's attention toward the One who really understands the longing of his heart. Too many men grow up believing that the inconsolable ache in his heart is for "a woman." To love a woman, get married, and then have children is thought to be the only script that will satisfy his heart's deepest longing. But no man, woman, or child can appease this longing; it can only be satisfied by the ultimate lover of our soul—Christ Jesus. This book nudges a man closer to God, while acknowledging any longing he may have to be loved and cherished by a woman.

The Right Guy for the Right Girl is not about finding the right woman, but being the right man.

Thus it focuses on ten qualities of a godly man that are found in the Book of Ruth and other Scriptures. These qualities will not only enhance your relationship with your heavenly Lover, but also guide you as a single man, guard you while you date, support you in marriage, and comfort you if you are ever widowed or divorced. What are *you* waiting for? Is it for that perfect job, the ideal relationship, a home, a career, a child? What if you get what you are waiting for? Will it truly bring the fullness of joy you long for? Anything other than a love relationship with the Lord Jesus Christ, regardless of how good that thing may be, will bring you discouragement and disillusionment. So come and explore the Word of God and learn what it really means to be a godly man, to be "the Right Guy."

For two decades I have been teaching the principles from *Lady in Waiting.* I have been asked thousands of times, "Where is the guy version of this timeless message?" Finally, The **Right Guy for the Right Girl** will be available for the instruction and encouragement of thousands of guys who know that they have been called to "live like sons of a King."

After publishing *Lady in Waiting,* I spent hundreds of hours looking at the leading man in the book of Ruth—Boaz—and wondering about his evil counterpart—*Bozo*. When searching the Scriptures for a perfect prototype of a Bozo in the Bible, I found a "prince" who did not act like the son of a King. Hence, Prince Amnon became the poster child of the "Bozo guy" in the Scriptures. *Amnon* in Hebrew means "trustworthy," but prince Amnon did not live his name. In fact, Prince Amnon raped the beautiful, virgin sister of Absalom (see 2 Samuel 13). This is a powerful demonstration of a guy who **does not live his name.** Although Amnon's behavior is quite extreme—there are too many guys in the world who claim to be "sons of the King" but they **do not live their name**—a prince from an unshakeable kingdom.

I believe the leading male character in the Book of Ruth—Boaz—is not a rare example to be isolated and ignored but a challenge for all of God's sons to consider and imitate. Boaz's behavior in Chapter 2 of the Book of Ruth is enough for all of God's sons to focus on and imitate. If a guy like Boaz would begin to consider that God has called him to protect women and not use and dispose of them like paper cups—the Bozo tribe would shrink and the *Boaz tribe* would flourish.

The **Right Guy for the Right Girl** can be achieved even in the twenty-first century. This book will challenge you with principles that will fortify your capacity to be a son of God **who lives his name**—a prince from an unshakeable kingdom—a brave warrior who resists the exploitation of women and accepts the challenge to be a protector of God's girls in his world.

At a college event at the University of South Carolina—just before I was going to speak, a sharp young man approached me. He was smiling ear to ear and he said, "I have read your book *Lady in Waiting* and so have all my suite mates." Now I was a little stunned; he was the first guy I had met who had read *Lady in Waiting.* I asked him how he ended up reading the book. He smiled and said, "When my girlfriend broke up with me, she handed me a copy of your book and told me, "Read it and then you will understand why I broke up with you." Well, I did my best to stand composed and not laugh at his reply. Then he said, "I am so glad I read that book—now I know what I want in a woman and what I need to be to get such a woman."

I never forgot that conversation and I realized that this young man learned something about being *The Right Guy for the Right Girl* by reading *Lady in Waiting.* Now more guys will have a chance to learn and be guided by such timeless principles as becoming God's best to attract God's best!

CHAPTER 1

MAN OF RECKLESS
ABANDONMENT

The big day is over. Your roommate married a wonderful girl and you were the best man. You shared your roommate's joy, but now you wrestle with envy's painful grip. As the happy couple drives to the perfect honeymoon, you sit alone in an empty apartment, drowning your envy and self-pity with a pizza and video games.

Does this scenario sound familiar?

Have you assumed that your ultimate fulfillment would be found in marriage? Have you privately entertained the notion that the only satisfied men are married men? Have you been expecting your career to be the other main source of your satisfaction? If you have answered yes to any of these questions, then you have a prospect of disillusionment looming in the future. A man is not born a man. He is a man when he becomes what God wants him to be. This priceless truth can help keep your perspective clear in relation to true fulfillment in life. Too many Christian men think that the inner longings of their hearts relate only to love, marriage, family, and career. Look a little closer and see if that longing isn't ultimately for Jesus. Jackie heard Gary Chapman speak at a church one Sunday. He said, "I feel very strongly that marriage is not a higher calling than the single state. Happy indeed are those people, married or single, who have discovered that happiness is not found in marriage but in a right relationship with God." Fulfillment for a Christian man begins with the Lordship of Christ in every area of his life.

Are you still convinced that having Miss Right will chase away the blues? That's not surprising. The concept of Mr. or Miss Right has become a cliché in our society. Such a mind-set bombards singles daily. How can you renew your mind and rise above this stereotype? You can be an exception through understanding "the secret of the alabaster box."

The Secret of the Alabaster Box

In the days Jesus was on earth, when a young woman reached the age of availability for marriage, her family would purchase an alabaster box for her and fill it with precious ointment. The size of the box and the value of the ointment would parallel her family's wealth. This alabaster box would be part of her dowry. When a young man came to ask for her in marriage, she would respond by taking the alabaster box and breaking it at his feet. This gesture of anointing his feet showed him honor.

One day, when Jesus was eating in the house of Simon the leper, a woman came in and broke an alabaster box and poured the valuable ointment on Jesus' head (see Mark 14:3-9). The passage in Luke 7 that refers to this event harshly describes the woman as *"a woman in the city who was a sinner"* (Luke 7:37). This woman found Jesus worthy of such sacrifice and honor. In fact, Jesus memorialized her gesture in Matthew 26:13 (see also Mark 14:9). This gesture had such meaning, for not only did she anoint Jesus for burial, she also gave her all to a heavenly Bridegroom. Yes, she was a sinner (Who isn't, according to Romans 3:23?), but this sinner had dreams and wisely broke her alabaster box in the presence of the only One who can make any man or woman's dreams come true.

As the Church is the Bride of Christ (see Rev. 21:2,9), all members of the Body, both male and female, are called to give the best they have to honor Him. For a man, being part of the heavenly "Bride" simply means that you are called to an intimate relationship with and increasing knowledge of God.

What is in your alabaster box? Is your box full of fantasies that began as a little boy while you listened to bedtime stories, watched movies, or daydreamed about your future? Have you been holding on tightly to your alabaster box of dreams, frantically searching for a woman worthy of breaking your box? Take your alabaster box to Jesus and break it in His presence, for He is worthy of such honor. Having responded to the heavenly lover of your soul in such a manner, you can wait with confident assurance that, if it be God's will, He will provide you with an earthly bride.

How do you know if you have broken your alabaster box at the feet of Jesus? Such a decision will be reflected in reckless abandonment to the Lordship of Jesus Christ. When the Lord gives you a difficult assignment, such as another dateless month, you receive His terms without resentment. Your attitude will reflect Mary's response to the angel when she, as a single woman, was given a most difficult assignment. Mary said, *"I belong to the Lord, body and soul...let it happen as you say..."* (Luke 1:38 Phillips). Take your alabaster box, with your body, soul, and dreams, and entrust them to Jesus. When He is your Lord, you can joyfully walk in the path of life that He has for you.

Ruth's Reckless Abandonment

In the Book of Ruth, a young widow made a critical decision to turn her back on her people, her country, and her gods because her thirsty soul had tasted of the God of Israel. With just a "taste," she recklessly abandoned herself to the only true God. She willingly broke her alabaster box and followed the Lord wherever He would lead her.

But Ruth said, "Do not urge me to leave you or turn back from following

you; for where you go, I will go, and
where you lodge, I will lodge. Your
people shall be my people, and your
God, my God" (Ruth 1:16).

As you look at the following three areas of Ruth's life that were affected by her reckless abandonment to God, consider the parallels to your own price tag of commitment to God. Have you broken the valuable alabaster box yet?

New Friends

When Ruth told Naomi, *"Your people shall be my people,"* she understood that she would not be able to grow closer to the God of Israel if she remained among the Moabites (her own people). Ironically, God called Moab His washbasin (see Ps. 60:8; 108:9). One rinses dirt off in a wash-basin. Ruth chose to leave the washbasin and head for Bethlehem, which means the "house of bread."[1]

Even today there exist "Moabites" who will undermine your growth if you spend too much time with them. Sometimes mediocre Christians resist the zeal and commitment of a dedicated single man. Realizing that your friends drive you either toward or away from God, you may need to find a "new people" who will encourage your growth and not hinder it. *"He who walks with the wise grows wise, but a companion of fools suffers harm"* (Prov. 13:20 NIV).

Often the choice for deeper commitment produces resentment from people who were once "such good friends." Do not be alarmed; you are in good company. When the woman broke the alabaster box and poured it on Jesus, the disciples did not applaud her act of worship. Instead, with indignation they responded, *"Why this waste?"* (Matt. 26:8). The disciples of Jesus were filled with indignation because the woman had obviously wasted the ointment. But from a heavenly perspective, the great cloud of witnesses rejoiced as they beheld the woman giving such honor to Jesus. The broken alabaster box publicly evidenced the woman's reckless abandonment to Jesus. Is there such evidence in your daily life?

This is not to advocate that you distance yourself from all who have not broken their alabaster box at the feet of Jesus. Just consider the ultimate influence your friends have on your commitment to the Lordship of Jesus Christ. Be careful if you spend most of your free time with a friend who does not share your commitment to Jesus. It can affect your relationship with the Lord. If a non-Christian or a lukewarm Christian influences you rather than you influencing them, you may be headed for serious trouble. You mirror those who influence you. When a man stops growing spiritually, the lack of progress can often be traced back to a friendship that undermined his commitment to Jesus.

Take a moment to think about the spiritual depth of the friend who influences you the most. Is he daily becoming all that Jesus desires? If so, his growth will challenge you to grow. On the other hand, his apathy may ultimately be contagious. *"Do not be deceived: 'Bad company corrupts good morals'"* (1 Cor. 15:33). Have any of your friendships caused your spiritual life to go into a deep freeze?

Maybe you, like Ruth, need to distance yourself from those who, spiritually speaking, are more like a washbasin than a house of bread. The friends who influence you the most should be men who live by Hebrews 10:24 NIV: *"And let us consider how we may spur one another on toward love and good deeds."* Your best friends should be cheering you on in your commitment to Jesus.

New Surroundings

Ruth had to relocate in order to be fed spiritually. Likewise, some single men may have to "relocate" because some of their former relationships keep them in a constant state of spiritual "hunger." They have to change jobs or even their church in order to continue to grow. In the same way, be open to a change that may benefit your spiritual growth. Like Ruth, look for something that will stimulate your growth in the Lord.

A young man may be called to spend his summer ministering to a volleyball team instead of being in a discipleship group, but the commitment to do as the Lord directs is the key.

Ruth moved from a hedonistic society into a culture that attempted to please the God of the universe rather than the sensuous gods of the flesh. Within our advanced society of the twenty-first century, we often encounter men engaged in becoming a part of self-serving singles' clubs, singles' dating services, singles' cruises, singles' meet market—all created to keep singles busy in the waiting time of life. A committed single man must be sensitive to the inevitable challenges he will meet in his attempt to live unselfishly in such a self-serving society.

Unfortunately, our self-centered culture in America has penetrated the Church so much that a young man not only has to choose against the American culture, but sometimes against the more subtle, worldly Christian subculture tainting the Body of Christ.

Part of reckless abandonment is realizing how much our culture has affected our behavior patterns. Perhaps you want to be Christlike, but your lifestyle is a reflection of *Esquire* magazine or *GQ* rather than a new creation in Christ. A.W. Tozer said, "A whole new generation of Christians has come up believing that it is possible to 'accept' Christ without forsaking the world."[2] Ruth had to forsake the familiar and comfortable in order to receive God's best for her life.

New Faith

Ruth moved from a false religion into the only true and eternal relationship. Too many men have been involved in a form of religious worship, but have never had a vital, growing relationship with Jesus. Has your religious experience been like Isaiah 29:13b NIV? *"...Their worship of Me is made up only of rules taught by men."* Has your faith been a lifeless ritual rather than a vital love relationship with Jesus? Why not spend some of your free hours as a single man beginning a journey away from rituals into a deep relationship with Jesus Christ?

Do you know more about pleasing a girlfriend than you do about pleasing the Lord Jesus?

Dividends From a High Price

Ruth's choice was costly, but the return on this high price far outweighed her investment. Matthew 19:29 NIV says, *"And everyone who has left houses or brothers or sisters or father or mother or children or fields for My sake will receive a hundred times as much and will inherit eternal life."* Ruth made the choice to turn her back on all that was familiar and begin a whole new life. Her *"hundred times as much"* was a godly husband, a son who would be the grandfather of King David, and inclusion in the lineage of Jesus Christ. She turned her back on all that was familiar, and God rewarded Ruth's critical choice.

Another costly aspect of Ruth's choice was the time frame in Israel's history. It was the age of the judges, a period of time described as "do your own thing"; *Everyone did what was right in his own eyes* (Judg. 21:25b). Ruth chose not only to break her family cycle, but also to challenge the lifestyle that many in Israel embraced. She wanted God's will, not hers; His blueprints, not her elementary scribbling; God's assignment, not her foolish plans.

Whenever a single man decides to abandon himself completely to Jesus, as Ruth did, he will find himself out of step with society and, sometimes, even with his friends. A single man today needs the boldness to challenge and break the cycle of the "American way" that exalts a relationship with a woman as the answer to life. This "American way" blurs the reality of the ultimate answer to life found in a deep relationship with Jesus Christ. Author M. Denis de Rougemont recently quoted C.S. Lewis, who said, "the conjugal eros 'ceases to be a devil only when it ceases to be a god.'"[3]

The Missing Puzzle Piece

Often a man will attempt to find delight in a career. In time, even his "great career" will prove to be less than satisfying. Neither a career nor marriage is enough to totally satisfy you. God knows that you will never be complete until you really understand that you are complete in Jesus. Colossians 2:9-10 says, *"For in Him all the fullness of Deity dwells in bodily form, and in Him you have been made complete, and He is the head over all rule and authority."* When a single man enters a career or even marriage without understanding that he is complete in Christ, he will be disillusioned and dissatisfied.

Incompleteness is not the result of being single, but of not being full of Jesus. Only in the process of reckless abandonment to Jesus does any man ever finally understand that, in Him, he is complete. When two "incomplete" singles get married, their union will not make them complete. Their marriage will be simply two "incomplete" people trying to find completeness in one another. Only when they understand that their fullness is found in a relationship with Jesus will they ever begin to *complement* one another. They can never *complete* one another. You were not created to complete another, but to *complement*. Completion is Jesus' responsibility, and complementing is a man's privilege. A man not complete in Jesus will be a drain on his wife. Such a man will expect his wife to fill the gap that only Jesus can fill. Only the single man who understands this means of being complete in Jesus is mature enough to be a spouse. *"For in Christ all the fullness of the Deity lives in bodily form, and you have been given fullness in Christ..."* (Col. 2:9-10 NIV). Are you feeling full yet? Ask the Lord right now to begin this process of revealing to your heart the reality of your fullness in Him. *"But it is good for me to draw near to God..."* (Ps. 73:28a KJV).

In her book *Loneliness*, Elisabeth Elliot states, "Marriage teaches us that even the most intimate human companionship cannot satisfy the deepest places of the heart. Our hearts are lonely "'til they rest in Him."[4] Elisabeth Elliot has been married three times (twice widowed), and she knows from experience that marriage does not make one complete; only Jesus does.

Satisfied by a Heavenly Lover

Does your relationship with Jesus reflect reckless abandonment to Him, or does it reflect only tokenism, a superficial effort toward following Jesus? Are you content to offer to Jesus that which cost you nothing? Are you influencing those around you to consider a life-changing commitment to Jesus Christ? In the Song of Solomon, the Shulammite was so committed to the one she loved that other women wanted to meet him. They were anxious to go with her to seek for him. *"Where has your lover gone, most beautiful of women? Which way did your lover turn, that we may look for him with you?"* (Song of Sol. 6:1 NIV). Who was this one so worthy of such reckless abandonment? Does your commitment to Jesus cause those around you to seriously consider whether Jesus is Lord of their lives? Or does your "token" relationship leave you and others still thirsty?

The depth of your relationship with God is up to you. God has no favorites; the choice to surrender is yours. A.W. Tozer so brilliantly stated in his book *The Pursuit of God:* "It will require a determined heart and more than a little courage to wrench ourselves loose from the grip of our times and return to biblical ways."[5]

Ruth had just such a determined heart, and the Lord honored her faith to move away from all that was familiar and take a journey toward the completely unknown. Ruth did not allow her friends, her old surroundings, or her culture's dead faith to keep her from running hard after God. She did not use the excuse of a dark past to keep her from a bright future that began with her first critical choice: reckless abandonment to Jesus Christ.

Have you made this critical choice, or have you settled for a mediocre relationship with Jesus? Amy Carmichael, one of the greatest single missionaries who ever lived, once remarked, "The saddest thing one meets is the nominal Christian."[6]

Choose right now to put mediocrity behind you; courageously determine to pursue Jesus with your whole heart, soul, and mind. As a single man, this is the perfect moment to establish a radical relationship with Jesus and remove any tokenism from your Christian walk.

Becoming the Right Guy begins with reckless abandonment to Jesus. The strength and discipline necessary to be a man of diligence, faith, virtue, devotion, purity, security, contentment, conviction, and patience is discovered in this radical way of relating to your heavenly lover. If you find yourself struggling with any of the qualities discussed in the following chapters, you may want to reexamine your own commitment to Jesus. Is it real and all-encompassing or merely ornamental? Do you remember a time when you broke your "alabaster box" in the presence of the Lord Jesus? The Right Guy understands the pleasing aroma of the perfume that flows from one's "broken alabaster box." It is the irresistible aroma of reckless abandonment to Jesus Christ.

Becoming a Man of Reckless Abandonment

From your perspective, what is the difference between "token commitment" and "reckless abandonment" to Jesus? Is your relationship with Jesus one of sacrifice or convenience? (Compare 1 Samuel 13:7b-14; 1 Samuel 15:24:30-31; and 2 Samuel 24:24.)

Have you broken your "alabaster box" at the feet of Jesus? (See Mark 14:3-9 and Luke 7:36-39.) Are you afraid to break your box at His feet? Why?

_____

_____

_____

How has your relationship with Jesus affected your friends, your surroundings, and your faith? (See Matthew 19:29.)

_____

_____

_____

Read Colossians 2:10. What does being "complete" (KJV) in Jesus mean to you? In what ways do you feel incomplete? How can that be changed? It is important to understand that you are complete in Him before you marry.

_____

_____

_____

_____

_____

Endnotes

1. *Scofield Bible* (New York: Oxford University Press, 1967), 51, note on Genesis 35:19.
2. A.W. Tozer, *The Pursuit of God* (Camp Hill, PA: Christian Publishing Inc., 1982), 16.
3. C.S. Lewis, *The Collected Works of C.S. Lewis; Christianity and Culture* (New Jersey: Inspirational Press, Edison, 1996), 197.
4. Elisabeth Elliot, *Loneliness* (Nashville, TN: Oliver Nelson, 1988), 16.
5. Tozer, *The Pursuit of God*, 29.
6. Quoted in Elisabeth Elliot, *A Chance to Die* (Old Tappan, NJ: Fleming H. Revell Company, 1987), 117.

CHAPTER 2

MAN OF DILIGENCE

While getting ready for a speaking engagement, she managed to get the kids up, dressed, and fed; fill the lunch boxes; load everyone in the car; and take them to school. Then she hurried home to set her hair and do her makeup. Finally dressed and ready to go speak, she made one last dash for the bathroom. While washing her hands, she noticed that the toilet was overflowing—not a slow drip, but pouring out all over the floor and into her open-toed shoes and nylons. She scrambled for towels and used them to build a dike then rubbed her feet dry and squirted her shoes with perfume. She ran out the door and jumped into the car. Halfway to the church she realized that she had left her Bible and outlines on the kitchen counter.

Such is the drama of Jackie Kendall's daily life. This kind of insanity is not unique to her. Every wife and mother daily deals with the legitimate needs of her husband and children. These needs take precedence over anything she might want to do, regardless of how "noble" her desires are! To be involved in the simplest form of ministry may require the married woman three times as much time to accomplish, in comparison to the single woman. Although a single woman may long for the "chaos" of a family, she must not waste her time wishing for it. She must be diligent to use her single time wisely now. She has more control over her time and choices now than she will probably ever have again. (The single parent is not included in this comparison because her responsibilities are double that of a married woman. She must go "solo" in raising children, increasing the burden of her daily priorities even more.)

The perfect time to make the most of every opportunity is while you are single. Every believer should use time wisely, as Ephesians 5:15-17 NIV says: *"Be very careful, then, how you live—not as unwise but as wise, making the most of every opportunity, because the days are evil. Therefore do not be foolish, but understand what the Lord's will is."*

John Fischer wrote this:

God has called me to live now. He wants me to realize my full potential as a man right now, to be thankful about where I am, and to enjoy it to the fullest. I have a strange feeling that the single person who is always wishing he were married will probably get married, discover all that is involved, and wish he were single again! He will ask himself, "Why didn't I use that time for the Lord when I didn't have so many other obligations? Why didn't I give myself totally to Him when I was single?"[1]

The single man can be involved in the Lord's work on a level that a married man cannot because of the distractions and responsibilities of being a husband and father. Ironically, some single men can be so distressed by their single state that they become emotionally more distracted than a husband and father of four children.

Rather than staying home worrying about another "dateless" Saturday night, realize how much valuable time has been entrusted to you at this point in your life. Rather than resent your many single hours, embrace them as a gift from God—a package that contains opportunities to serve Him that are limited only by your own self-pity and lack of obedience.

No Time to Waste

Understanding God's promised provision for widows, Naomi sent Ruth to gather grain in the field of a kinsman. Ruth was willing to use her life working diligently at whatever her Lord called her to do. She would not be paralyzed by her lack of a husband. *"And Ruth the Moabitess said to Naomi, 'Please let me go to the field and glean among the ears of grain after one in whose sight I may find favor.' And she said to her, 'Go, my daughter'"* (Ruth 2:2). She also did not allow the fact that she was a stranger from Moab to cause her to fear while she was gleaning in a strange field. Ruth was the "new girl in town," an obvious newcomer, but she was not afraid to walk into a totally unfamiliar situation. Nor did Boaz hold back from showing kindness to a foreign worker in his fields who was a stranger to Bethlehem and Israel. Countless single men stay home rather than travel alone into the unknown. They not only miss out on being encouraged by others, but also are not exposed to new relationships when they remain at home tied up by cords of fear and feeling sorry for themselves.

If a single man allows the fearful prospect of meeting new people and new challenges to keep him at home, he may find himself bored and lonely while all the time missing many satisfying and fulfilling experiences. Don't stay home as a fearful single man. Take that step of faith and volunteer. Get involved and see what you have been missing. One single said, "Serving the Lord brings such inexpressible joy." People who are not involved in serving the Lord obviously have never experienced this joy; otherwise churches wouldn't have to beg them to get involved. If all the singles in the church just realized their "strategic position," churches would not ever need to ask for help with children, youth, or college students. There would probably be so many available single workers that there would be a "surplus of manpower"!

Free to Follow

Are you busy serving Jesus during your free time, or do you waste hours trying to pursue and snag an available girl? Ruth was a widow, but when she and Naomi moved back to Bethlehem, Ruth did not waste a moment feeling sorry for herself. She went right to work. Instead of being drained by her discouraging circumstances, she took advantage of them and diligently embraced each day.

Ruth came to the God of Israel after years of living in darkness, but He gladly received her service even though she was a Moabite foreigner. She bound herself to the service of the Lord, interweaving her service with Him like the braiding of a heavy rope. Isaiah 56:6-7 NIV refers to foreigners binding themselves to the Lord and Him willingly receiving their "diligent" service: *"And foreigners who bind themselves to the Lord to serve Him...these I will bring to My holy mountain...."*

Are you tightly bound to the Lord, serving Him diligently, or has your relationship and service been unraveling over the years as you continue to be single and not married? Has resentment and self-pity unraveled what used to be a tightly woven labor for the Lord? You must be sensitive to the things and situations that distract you from redeeming your free time. "Whatever might blur the vision God had given [Elisabeth Elliot] of His work, whatever could distract or deceive or tempt others to seek anything but the Lord Jesus Himself she tried to eliminate."[2]

Some singles see the lack of a mate as God denying them something for a more "noble purpose"—*a cross to bear!* Our selfish nature tends to focus on what we do not have rather than on what we do have—free time—that can be used for others and ourselves. Is your life on hold until you have someone to hold?

Sitting in a restaurant across from a beautiful blonde, as the woman's personal story began to unfold, the listener was somewhat overwhelmed. Here was a very attractive woman who had put her life with Jesus on hold after her world fell apart. She had been married for a few years and was trying to conceive a child, when she heard her single best friend was pregnant. What irony: her unmarried friend was with child and she remained childless. The irony turned into a trauma when this married woman found out that the father was her own husband. Can you imagine the devastation this caused in this beautiful young woman's heart? Have you experienced such a crushing emotional blow? The stunned listener began to cry out for wisdom concerning this tragedy. Jesus reminded the listener that God is not intimidated by trauma. In fact, Psalm 34:18 says, *"The Lord is near to the brokenhearted, and saves those who are crushed in spirit."* This brokenhearted woman had put her life on hold after her husband divorced her. Such a response is understandable, but that day in the restaurant, this now-single woman decided to take her broken heart, her empty arms, and her loneliness and give them to Jesus. In exchange, Jesus taught her how to resist feeling sorry for herself and how to stop living in the arena of bitterness. After she made the choice of recklessly abandoning herself to Jesus as Lord, she was free to serve Him. This once-brokenhearted single woman has been transformed into a fearless servant of the Lord. In fact, she became a missionary to Quito, Ecuador.

Have you also put your life on hold? Do you have an excuse for not serving Jesus?

Some men put their lives on hold, waiting for some girl to come into their lives. They cannot comprehend fullness and satisfaction without a woman. These men have settled for the "generic" version of life. How unlike Jesus' statement in John 10:10, in which He said He came so we might have a more abundant life. Do you believe that the abundant life is only for the married man? Do you think that a man with a wife, two children, a nice home, and two insurance policies is more satisfied with life than you are? Life is satisfying only when you diligently serve the Lord, whatever your circumstances.

Enviable Singleness

Singleness is an enviable condition. An unmarried man has something that a married man gives up on his wedding day: extra time for Jesus. Too many young men waste valuable years as they wait for life to begin—after marriage or succeeding at a career. They rarely realize the priceless free time they waste until it is gone. Have you neglected some mission or ministry opportunities because you feared prolonging your unmarried state?

If you love serving Jesus, please do not waste any of the free time you have. Do not consider yourself too unhappy to help anyone else. Self-centeredness will rob you of the joy of serving. Satan, who is effective at distracting you from God's best, wants you to continue dreaming about how "one day" you will get involved in ministry. He wants to sidetrack you from making a lasting investment. Too many men foolishly believe his lies. Therefore, they lose sight of opportunities to get involved in any form of outreach to others.

Unsatisfied and unfulfilled, they sink deep into the quicksand of "maybe next year."

Many have embraced the ultimate deception, "Poor me." An excerpt from a single friend's letter exposes this self-pitying lie:

> As is usually the case, as soon as I stopped asking what was in it for me and began asking what I was meant to give, things began to improve, beginning with my attitude. I continue to grow and be greatly strengthened in my relationship with God one-on-one and to seek out where I can serve those around me.

This single has learned how to use free time for Jesus rather than sitting at home writing melancholy poetry.

Unrelenting Pursuit

Undistracted and *unrelenting* describe different facets of the word *diligence*. The Man of Diligence embodies these terms. A verse that describes his attitude toward ministry and service is First Corinthians 15:58 NIV: *"Therefore, my dear brothers, stand firm. Let nothing move you. Always give yourselves fully to the work of the Lord, because you know that your labor in the Lord is not in vain."* Do these terms describe your attitude and approach to using your free time for Jesus? Let's examine how diligence affects every aspect of your service and ministry for the Lord.

Diligence and the Ministry of Teaching

Have you been diligently pursuing truth for years, but not giving out as much as you have taken in? Are you involved in a regular Bible study where you give, maybe even teach? Almost as dangerous as neglecting the Word is the habit of taking it in but not putting it into practice. "Impression without expression can lead to depression." Do you keep attending church, Sunday school, Bible studies, seminars, and retreats—taking yet never giving? Take advantage of this time in your life when you can be involved in teaching without so many encumbrances. Maybe you've considered leading a discipleship group. Hesitate no more; go for it! There is no time in your life more perfect than now. Maybe you have toyed with the idea of teaching a Bible study. Do not delay. The future may hold more distractions that would continue to keep you from your goal.

Diligence and the Ministry of Encouragement

How many times a week do you find yourself in a position where someone has shared a need with you and you want so much to respond with wisdom and grace? Isaiah 50:4 NIV says, *"The Sovereign Lord has given me an instructed tongue, to know the word that sustains the weary. He wakens me morning by morning, wakens my ear to listen like one being taught."* Do you have a hard time responding to such an early morning wake-up call? Rising early to develop the tongue of a disciple will open a door of ministry to those who are weary, whether they are at work, at church, or even at the grocery store. Your very words will be a ministry of healing and encouragement. *"The tongue that brings healing is a tree of life, but a deceitful tongue crushes the spirit"* (Prov. 15:4) NIV. Such predawn training will give you the privilege of becoming God's garden hose in a land of many thirsty people.

Diligence and the Ministry of Prayer

Do you have a prayer partner? If you do not, ask the Lord right now for such a gift. A prayer partner can help you pray for others. Of course, this prayer partner needs to be a male, one who can encourage you to keep God's perspective on your commitment to being all God wants you to be, whether married or single.

"A prayer partnership serves as one of the greatest assets for accomplishing the deepest and highest work of the human spirit: prayer."[3] Praying regularly with someone (or a small group) is such a vital part of your service to God. To intercede on behalf of someone else's need is a privilege. When you intercede with a partner, the "duet" of harmony before God can change your world. Matthew 18:19 NIV describes this harmonious duet: *"Again, I tell you that if two of you on earth agree about anything you ask for, it will be done for you by My Father in heaven."* That little verb *agree* refers to harmony. Do you have someone with whom you can prayerfully approach God in harmony? Rather than searching for a life-partner, look for a prayer partner. Together you can participate in God-given prayer projects. Together you can discover how you can take your concerns for others and turn them into prayer projects.

Diligence and the Ministry of Service

It is doubtful that there could ever be a better time to serve Jesus than this "moment" of singleness. Rather than wasting precious moments fantasizing about an earthly lover, take advantage of your free hours each day to serve the Lord of Heaven. If you are frustrated and distracted, rather than fruitfully serving Jesus, then ask Him right now to adjust your vision.

As Ruth diligently worked at what she could, God sent her a spouse. Boaz was an older man (see Ruth 3:10) who waited patiently and did not marry until God sovereignly brought Ruth to his threshing floor. God will do the same for you if that is His plan. Is there a ministry opportunity you should be working with? Why not consider a short-term mission trip? Don't worry about that certain girl you have had your eye on for a while. If she is God's best for you, she will be there when you return. Your single state may not be permanent, but it definitely is not to be a comatose state until your princess arrives. Is there an opportunity of service that you have avoided because you can't give up your search for your princess? Is there an application for a summer ministry waiting for you to fill out? Such a chance may come again next summer, but then it will be even harder to respond to the prospect of serving, for time brings more and more distractions. As you get older, you assume more obligations and responsibilities that demand your time and attention. Such distractions will make serving Jesus even more difficult. Have you given Jesus full reign over your time?

Limitless ministry opportunities exist for the Man of Diligence. These ministries are available right this moment. They do not demand a Bible college education. The only requirement is a single man who desires to use his time wisely in ministry.

Diligence and the Ministry of Writing

This ministry requires pen and paper—or e-mail, online chats, and social networks—and a willing heart. Much of the New Testament was originally written as letters to believers. An encouraging letter or text message can be read and re-read. So often a person will think about writing someone, but the thought never becomes action. You may ignore the inward suggestion because of a busy schedule or a resistance to writing. A personal note or e-mail, though, serves as oxygen to the soul of the recipient. *"He who refreshes others will himself be refreshed"* (Prov. 11:25b NIV).

If you are not comfortable writing a full letter, or your schedule does not permit such a ministry in writing, then purchase some pre-stamped postcards and try to send them regularly to different people who need a refreshing word. Or make time to regularly send a few e-mails or text messages. The Lord wants you to be involved in the lives of those around you, and writing is one of those opportunities.

Diligence and the Ministry of Listening

A ministry of listening is available right now. When someone is grieving, your presence provides more power than words. When someone is burdened, you may want to just listen and silently pray rather than verbally give the solution to the problem. Being content to listen to someone today is a gift you can give. A listener provides a healing audience for someone who is hurting. When Jackie's sister died, listeners who allowed her to share the loss and cry freely were God's greatest source of comfort. Being content to listen is a gift you can give to someone today.

It may take a gentle touch to minister to the spirit. It also may require just being with the person, whether standing for hours in a hospital hallway or sitting by a sickbed. Sometimes even the greatest songs or truths are not the appropriate thing during a crisis. *"Like one who takes away a garment on a cold day, or like vinegar poured on soda, is one who sings songs to a heavy heart"* (Prov. 25:20 NIV). This ministry requires not seminary training, but a loving, listening heart.

Diligence and the Ministry of Hospitality

The ministry of hospitality is a way to share Christ's love and graciousness with others. Simply cooking for others—or, if you don't cook, delivering a restaurant meal or a dozen doughnuts—is a significant ministry, especially during illness or bereavement. Casseroles and cakes can be such a blessing to a new mother, an elderly neighbor, or someone emotionally devastated by a death in the family. What a way to share the love of Christ with someone who needs to see Christianity in action.

Please do not limit your ministry of hospitality to candlelight dinners for the woman of your dreams. Think how a sumptuous steak dinner for a group of single men, or even high school boys, could minister to them.

Diligence and the Ministry of Helps

This ministry requires time, but it is invaluable. Helping others with the "dailies" of life is a gift that breaks their exhausting monotony.

Helping a friend get his apartment ready for special guests, or helping him move into a new place, leaves the recipient grateful. Mere physical labor may seem so insignificant in comparison to church visitation, but the Word of God speaks clearly to such a misconception. *"Whether, then, you eat or drink or whatever you do, do all to the glory of God"* (1 Cor. 10:31). Maybe a friend needs a ride to the airport during rush hour, or maybe he needs his lawn mowed, or car repaired. These duties can all be done unto the Lord. *"Whatever you do, work at it with all your heart, as working for the Lord, not for men"* (Col. 3:23 NIV).

Non-Newsy Works

For those of you who are diligently going after Jesus and the privilege of serving Him, here is a very special reminder. Sometimes you will be called to do some monotonous work that will not make the headlines. It may frustrate you because it doesn't seem very "impressive." Consider the reality of all the non-newsy things Jesus did during most of His life (30 years), before He began His formal ministry. What more humbling work could Ruth have done than gathering leftover grain for the survival of her mother-in-law and herself? Richard Foster brilliantly penned this thought, "If all of our serving is before others, we will be shallow people indeed."[4] Jesus spoke clearly about the constant public display of our service. *"Everything they do is done for men to see..."* (Matt. 23:5 NIV). The next time someone asks you to help out in service that is monotonous and non-newsy, don't hesitate. The King records such works (see Matt. 25:34-35). Teaching Bible studies, going out on evangelism teams, mission trips, and even prayer groups—all these are priceless opportunities to serve, but they are not the only avenues. Serving in the preschool department at church, going to kids' camp, and even scrubbing toilets for a junior high banquet are all honorable services that the Man of Diligence can embrace with respect.

Look at your schedule and decide how some of your free time that was wasted yesterday might be redeemed today. Allow no more room in your schedule for distractions. Such wise use of your free time will give you the gift of "no regrets." Your future service will be focused and no longer wasted.

Free hours,
Not wasted by me,
using my free time,
To serve only Thee.

Realizing how temporary free time will be
Never to regret a missed opportunity,
For others to be blest,
Through yielded me.
JMK

Becoming a Man of Diligence

Determine what may have kept you from being more involved in ministry by seeing which of the following four characters you identify with the most.

JEALOUS JAMES: Do you focus on the gifts others have been given and, therefore never find your own niche in ministry? Have you unwisely compared yourself with other men? (See 1 Corinthians 4:7; 12:7; Romans 12:3.)

_____

_____

PRINCE PAUL: Do you want to serve God on your terms? Do you want to write the script and have the leading role? (See John 4:34; 7:16,18; Matthew 23:5.)

_____

_____

_____

FEARFUL FRANK: Do you fear what others think? Are you afraid of becoming too involved and being labeled a fanatic? Do you hesitate to be a Man of Diligence because you feel so inadequate? (See Proverbs 29:25; 2 Timothy 1:7; 1 Thessalonians 5:24.)

DOUBTING DAN: Faith is believing what God says about you. Do you long to become more involved in a number of ministries, but feel your faith will fizzle before you finish? Have you struggled with serving the Lord in the past, so you doubt yourself today? (Part of ministry is learning, so don't let yesterday's struggles prevent future successes.) (See 1 John 4:4; 2 Timothy 1:9; 1 Timothy 6:12.)

To get involved in any ministry demands a sacrifice. Have you allowed your self-centeredness to dominate your daily schedule? Inventory your past week and see how many activities you did for others. Or go through your checkbook tonight and see how many checks were written for things concerning others. (See 2 Samuel 24:24; Philippians 2:3-4; Matthew 19:29.)

Endnotes

1. John Fischer, *A Single Person's Identity* (Discovery Papers, Catalog No. 3154, August 5, 1973), 3.
2. Elisabeth Elliot, *A Chance to Die* (Old Tappan, NJ: Fleming H. Revell Company, 1987), 117.
3. Charles F. Stanley, *Handle With Prayer* (Wheaton, IL: Victory Books, 1982), 15.
4. Richard J. Foster, *Celebration of Discipline* (San Francisco: Harper & Row Publishers, 1978), 117.

CHAPTER 3

MAN OF FAITH

Faith...
a fruit whose blossoming aroma
Inspires one to victory,
and sustains one after loss.
JMK

I f you are spouse hunting, we have heard that Alaska, Montana, and Florida have an abundance of men. Proportionately, women most outnumber men in the Northeastern states.

Are you panicked because you are residing in one of the female-sparse states?

Do you live in a town or city where you need "eyes of faith" in relation to the prospects of a mate? Do you attend a church where the "pickin's are slim"? Let's take a closer look at two contrasting attitudes toward one's circumstances.

Where the Girls Are

Think back to how the love story in the Book of Ruth began. Three widows, Naomi with her two daughters-in-law, Orpah and Ruth, have just been through the painful experience of losing the men they loved. Just facing each day without their mates required much faith because of the difficulty in providing for one's own needs. Naomi, being a Jewess, made the decision to leave Moab and return to her hometown in Israel (Bethlehem). Her two daughters-in-law had become young widows, so she encouraged them to return to their families where they each might find another husband. Naomi's suggestion appeared very rational. Naomi knew that they (being Moabites) had a better chance of finding husbands in Moab than in Israel. *"...Go back, each of you, to your mother's home. May the Lord show kindness to you, as you have shown to your dead and to me. May the Lord grant that each of you will find rest in the home of another husband"* (Ruth 1:8-9 NIV). Would Ruth have ever found a believing husband to be united with if she had also returned to Moab?

Naomi lovingly pointed Orpah and Ruth in the direction of possible prospects. She actually encouraged them to go in a direction where they could *see* how they might each find a husband. Orpah followed Naomi's advice and chose logical sight for future direction. She gave Naomi a kiss goodbye and headed "where the boys are." Such "choices" are often based on logical sight and do not need even a mustard seed of faith.

Many single men spend their free time searching for the same kind of location chosen by Orpah. They attend schools because they can "see" the prospects. They join churches based on apparent ratios of women to men. They go to seminars, retreats, and conferences looking for the woman of their dreams.

Some men have changed churches because they were in a "no prospective mate" district. Others avoid churches understocked with available women. Can you relate? Some single women serve only one term on a mission field and never return because the ratio of available men to women shrinks even smaller on the mission field than in their home church. A single woman serving as a missionary wrote: "Well, here I am in a no-hope situation. There is only 1 single man to about 50 single women." Should single men and women focus on the situation or on the Sovereign One?

Chance Rendezvous

A man who takes the route of Orpah (sensual, logical sight) often invents ways for a "chance rendezvous" with the woman of his dreams. You can see him loitering in the very area that Miss Right regularly frequents, hoping that she might finally notice him and the romance will begin. This sounds more like a Harlequin romance. Such a young man might sing in the choir, not because he wants to make a joyful noise unto the Lord, but because he wants a weekly chance to sit near the prospect (single woman) that his "sensual sight" has focused upon. Such impure motives for such a noble cause!

If the Lord wants to give you a woman, He does not need your clever "chance rendezvous." This is not advocating that you avoid women completely and expect the Lord to "UPS" His choice to your front door. You need to participate in activities that involve men and women, but be sensitive to your motives whenever you find yourself in the presence of "available women." Consider this Scripture whenever checking your motives and your pulse! Proverbs 16:2 NIV says, *"All a man's ways seem innocent to him, but motives are weighed by the Lord."*

You can prevent disappointing moments if you check your heart whenever you go to a singles' activity. Much preparation (like taking a shower, putting on cologne, and choosing the perfect outfit) precedes one's attending such an activity, yet so little heart preparation does. The guy with sensual sight can become so obsessed with finding his girl that he neglects his inner self. Orpah's style (logical sight) tends to become the norm, but Ruth offers an alternative to this vain search for a spouse. She demonstrates what it means to be a person of faith.

Eyes of Faith

Orpah's example of going after the available men could have influenced Ruth to return to Moab, the home of her parents and the gods of her youth. Ruth, however, remained with Naomi and her God. Ruth certainly must have considered the probability of remaining single if she went with Naomi. Even though it promised no prospects of a husband, she chose to follow Naomi and her God back to Bethlehem. Ruth chose to trust God with her future. She looked not with sensual sight, but through "eyes of faith." Even though Ruth was young in her faith in the God of Israel, she chose to trust with her heart for the future her eyes could not yet see.

The International Children's Bible describes faith in this way: *"Faith means being sure of the things we hope for. And faith means knowing that something is real even if we do not see it"* (Heb. 11:1). This childlike expression of such an abstract quality can become a daily reality in the life of the Man of Faith. Your hope cannot be put in some dreamed-up future. It must be in the God who knows your past, present, and future, and loves you enough to give you the best.

Are you in what seems like a "no-hope situation"? Maybe you are attending a church that requires you to exercise faith to even open the door and go in, since every woman there is either married, engaged, or the age of your baby sister. Instead of becoming fearful during this trying situation, look to the Lord through "eyes of faith." To do so brings God great pleasure. Hebrews 11:6a says, *"And without faith it is impossible to please* [totally satisfy] *Him...."* Your daily use of "eyes of faith" brings Jesus such satisfaction.

Do you long to please Him? Then reconsider your circumstances and realize that what seems to be a hopeless situation (no prospects on the horizon) is just the flip side of the view through "eyes of faith."

Sometimes in an attempt to be a Man of Faith, one can get sidetracked trying to hurry the "female order delivery" process.

One must admit that it is more likely a man would find a godly woman in a church, at a Christian college, or in local Bible study. These are obviously good places to find Miss Right, but the assumption of finding her can result in disillusionment. Hundreds of wonderful single men live and breathe in all the right places, but they remain single.

You may wonder, "How can I be a Man of Faith when I feel so insecure deep in my heart that God will deliver the goods? What if I have faith in God and end up being 98 and unmarried?" Of course, you would never outright admit that you're not sure you can trust God.

That would appear too ungodly! But there's that sneaking fear in the back of your mind: "If I really give up my search and have 'eyes of faith,' God might not give me what I desire, like a wife and children." God knows when your heart aches for these things. But He also knows that these earthly things will not make you secure.

To be sure, your gnawing fears are very common. The enemy knows how common these fears are, and he feeds them by adding a few lies like, "If you give your desire to the Lord, He will send you to outer Bufelia where all the women are three feet tall," or, "If you give all your desires to the Lord, you might get married, but you'll definitely not want to take pictures of your fiancée for your friends to see."

"Can I really trust God with all my hopes and dreams? How will I meet Miss Right if I have eyes of faith? Doesn't God need any help in developing my dreams? What about needing to be in the right place at the right time? How will I meet Miss Right if I'm not out and about where she might be? I feel the urge to make a mad dash to the next party or to attend the college with the most available women." Such anxious thoughts are based on fears, not faith. "Faith does not eliminate questions. But faith knows where to take them."[1] You may say you have faith and are just being practical. Are you? What is the opposite of faith? Fear. Who knows that better than the enemy? At the base of his being is the desire to trick you into missing God's best. Satan wants you to believe the lie that cripples faith: God cannot be trusted.

In order to have "eyes of faith," you may have to use a spiritual eyewash to remove the debris that the enemy has dropped into your eyes. The Man of Faith will have times when his secure eyes of faith begin to blink into an anxious twitch of insecure, sensual sight. He can admit his insecurity to the Lord and He can calm the twitching eyes. Spending some quality time in the Word is the best "eyewash" for "eyes of faith."

Romans 10:17 says, *"So faith comes from hearing, and hearing by the word of Christ."* A Man of Faith may have to spend dateless weekends in female-saturated churches. He can only be content in this trying situation if he has his "eyes of faith" properly focused on the ultimate relationship—with his heavenly lover. Datelessness is a common type of debris that irritates the "eyes of faith," but the eyewash treatment— quality time with Jesus and reading His Word—is always effective.

Divine Encounter

In contrast to the manipulated "chance rendezvous" of Orpah, Ruth had a divine encounter that affected not only her marital status but also biblical history. That first morning in Bethlehem, Ruth happened to stop in a field belonging to Boaz. Interestingly enough, the same day, Boaz "just happened" to visit that very same field where Ruth was gathering the leftover grain. Their meeting was neither an accident nor the product of female maneuvering. Instead, it was the work of a sovereign God.

God providentially directed Ruth to the field of Boaz. You find this divine encounter in the second chapter of Ruth, verse 3: *"...and she happened to come to the portion of the field belonging to Boaz...."* The verb *happened* in Hebrew means "chanced upon." This leaves no room for manipulation. She had a chance, and her chance transported her into the center of God's will and right to Boaz's field. Boaz was wealthy and available. Ruth did not "have plans" when she chanced upon his field. Ruth's "eyes of faith" led her to the exact spot where she would meet her Mr. Right, Boaz, whose name means "pillar of strength." (Contrast the meaning of his name to that of her first husband, Mahlon, which means "weak and sickly"! God rewarded Ruth's faith with a husband who was a "pillar of strength.")

If Jesus wants you married, He will orchestrate the encounter. You have nothing to fear except getting in His way and trying to "write the script" rather than following His. Jesus does have your best interest at heart. He desires to bless you by giving you the best. Sometimes what you perceive as the best is nothing more than a generic version. Consider His wisdom and love in comparison to your own wisdom and self-love. In whom are you going to trust—all Wisdom and Everlasting Love or little ol' finite you? Ever since the Garden of Eden, men have often felt they could and should know as much as God. Much pain in our world has resulted from dependence on our wisdom rather than on our Father's.

Meeting Across Continents

A single man was serving the Lord in a foreign country. His "eyes of faith" sometimes twitched as the reality of no prospects, especially English-speaking ones, while he diligently served the Lord. At a Bible conference, he met a beautiful former airline stewardess who lived on the other side of the world. She had left her secular job and gone to Germany as a missionary. She was an unlikely candidate according to sensual sight and basic logic, but a long-distance courtship began and they eventually married. Today they serve the Lord together in the Philippines.

Your circumstances and geographical location do not threaten God's will and purpose. Just as God brought Eve to Adam, Rebekah to Isaac, Ruth to Boaz, and someday the Bride of Christ to Himself, He will one day bring Miss Right to you if you are to be married. This is true regardless of your unique situation. Your location or your occupation may not make you very accessible to available godly women, but these roadblocks do not handicap God. Time and time again, we have had the privilege of watching God bring a wonderful, godly girl into the life of a Man of Faith. She seems to suddenly appear out of nowhere.

God brought His best for one man all the way from Escondido, California, to Kenya, Africa. David met Vivian at a Bible study just before she left for Kenya to teach missionary kids. Had she not been leaving for Africa that week, they might have had time to become better acquainted. Frustrated by the reality of meeting such a fine

Christian woman just before she left to go half-way around the world, he followed the Lord with "eyes of faith." Little did he know the script God had written. Halfway through Vivian's first term on the field, David was sent on a construction team from the United States to do some work for the academy where she taught. He and Vivian not only got acquainted, but they also married right there in Kenya. Just as Jesus brought David to Vivian, Jesus can bring your life-mate to you, no matter where you live.

The ultimate demonstration of Men of Faith are the single men who have lived the ten principles in this book—and who themselves continue in a state of singleness. They have not numbed their longing to be married; instead, they have embraced their Lord so tightly that they face their prolonged singleness with peace, not bitterness.

Have you hesitated about taking a new job or even going to a foreign mission field because you might miss Miss Right? Have you passed up opportunities to serve in a Sunday school department because you might miss meeting the woman of your dreams? If you are trying to orchestrate the "divine encounter," you might be setting yourself up for a disappointing crash. Wherever you are, whatever your circumstances may be, whether divorced, widowed, or single and getting older every day, be assured that God has not lost your address or your file. He knows exactly where you are and what you need. Remember, God has already taken care of your greatest need—your salvation—and as Romans 8:32 reminds us, *"He who did not spare His own Son, but delivered Him over for us all, how will He not also with Him freely give us all things?"*

You make the most important decision in life, giving your life to Jesus Christ, "by faith." The second most important decision concerns your life-mate. This decision also demands the element of faith. Waiting for one's life-mate and then saying "I do" to her demands secure faith, like Ruth's faith in the God of Israel.

Before you read any further, if you have been full of doubts and anxiety in reference to your future mate, take a few moments to confess your doubts to God and ask His Spirit to develop in your life this quality of faith. Your faith during the "waiting period" pleases God.

Don't fear or resent the waiting periods in your life. These are the very gardens where the seeds of faith blossom. Whenever circumstances stimulate you to deepen your faith, don't resist them; instead embrace them willingly. Elisabeth Elliot said in *Passion and Purity* (a must-read for those who are having an anxiety attack during their extended waiting periods):

> I do know that waiting on God requires the willingness to bear uncertainty, to carry within oneself the unanswered question, lifting the heart to God about it whenever it intrudes upon one's thoughts.[2]

Whenever the "unanswered question" captures your mind or you are overtaken by the restlessness of singleness, take a moment to commit that care where it belongs. As First Peter 5:7 says, *"Casting all your anxiety on Him, because He cares for you."* This intruding anxiety about your lack of a life-mate is not reality, but rather a weakness that the Greater Reality is capable of handling. Just go to Jesus as soon as the intruder arrives. Such a practice will only enhance your life as a Man of Faith. Many single men have not recognized that the trying, frustrating waiting period is the perfect classroom for the Man of Faith. Don't skip class! Embrace those dateless nights and, by faith, rest in His faithfulness.

Becoming a Man of Faith

Browse through the Psalms, select several about trust and reliance, and circle the words *trust* and *rely* in red. Notice David's and other psalmists' trust in God. This exercise will strengthen your "eyes of faith." What are two other ways to strengthen your faith?

_____

_____

Read Romans 10:17 and Psalm 119. What are the parallels between a strong devotional life and being the Man of Faith?

_____

_____

Explain how you tend to manipulate your rendezvous with women and/or how you can allow God to be your heavenly dating service. Do you trust and believe Him to bring you the wife of His choice and in His perfect timing? Why or why not?

_____

_____

_____

Can you see how an extended period of single-ness serves as a great opportunity for you to develop into a Man of Faith? Explain.

_____

_____

_____

_____

_____

_____

_____

_____

_____

_____

Endnotes

1. Elisabeth Elliot, *A Chance to Die* (Old Tappan, NJ: Fleming H. Revell Company, 1987), 117.
2. Ibid., 59–60.

CHAPTER 4

MAN OF VIRTUE

Providing lasting pleasure,
potential beyond measure,
the rarest of treasure,
a reputation of virtuous character.
JMK

One of life's most costly and beautiful objects is born out of pain and irritation—the pearl. A tiny piece of sand slips into an oyster's shell and begins to rub against the soft tissue, causing irritation. In response to the irritation, the oyster produces a hard substance. This substance eventually develops into one of the world's most beautiful jewels—a lovely, luminous pearl. In fact, the greater the irritation, the more valuable the pearl!

Like the oyster, Joseph is an excellent male example of this metaphor:

> *Joseph named his older son Manasseh, for he said, "God has made me forget all my troubles and everyone in my father's family. Joseph named his second son Ephraim, for he said, 'God has made me fruitful in this land of my grief"* (Genesis 41:51,52).

Fruitfulness in grief (suffering) is possible but not without forgetting—letting go (forgiving) the past. For 18 years, the author, Jackie Kendall, has been wearing a bracelet with the name *Ephraim* on it, declaring to all that God can make you "fruitful in suffering." Now I see that Ephraim is only part of the healing equation. Manasseh—forgetting…letting go—requires forgiving the past and the people who form the painful past. Whenever you are facing grief or someone you love is facing grief/suffering—pray for the **blessing of Manasseh and Ephraim (Gen. 48:20).** When someone suffers, his view of God is sometimes blurred. *M & E* can help with adjusting your view so you end up with perfect vision—"50/20," as demonstrated in Genesis 50:20.

*"You intended to harm me, but God in-
tended it all for good. He brought me to
this position so I could save the lives of
many people"* (Genesis 50:20 NLT).

I know that 20/20 is perfect vision physically but 50/20 is perfect vision spiritually.

Like Ruth, Joseph looked toward the God of
Israel. He bravely faced the turmoil of change in
the direction of his life as well as a move to a foreign land, with the knowledge that he had been
betrayed by his own family. When he arrived in
that strange land, the trials did not end. But Joseph learned to be fruitful in a place of suffering
(Ephraim). Like Ruth, he was immediately thrown
into a new working situation among total strangers with new customs. Through all this stress, new
faith began to wrap itself around the painful situations. The by-product was a pearl of great value.

Joseph, betrayed by his family, became a
voice in the Pharoah's palace. He trusted God,
and God raised Him up to do mighty things
(see Genesis 41-45). God used Joseph to fulfill
a promise made to Abraham in Genesis 15:13
NIV: *"Then the LORD said to him, "Know for certain that your descendants will be **strangers** in a
country not their own, and they will be enslaved*

and mistreated four hundred years." Likewise, Ruth, widowed at a young age, chose to follow the God of Naomi, and found her place in the genealogy of the King of kings (see Matt. 1:5).

Many single men view themselves as ugly oyster shells lying on the beaches of life, beset with the trials and problems that come with not being married. To make matters worse, they compare their crusty exterior to all the attractive seashells around them and wonder how any woman could ever give her attention to them.

If you are one of these men, be encouraged. Don't view the trials of singleness as irritating grains of sand to be discarded as quickly as possible. Realize that God has them there to create something beautiful in you. James 1:2-4 says, *"Consider it all joy, my brethren, when you encounter various trials, knowing that the testing of your faith produces endurance. And let endurance have its perfect result, that you may be perfect and complete, lacking in nothing."*

God is using the sands of singleness to make you perfect and complete. He's developing pearls of character in your life. He knows that whatever you use to "catch" a girl, you must also use to keep her. If you attract a girl with only your looks, then you are headed for trouble, since looks don't last. As time goes on, we all end up looking like oysters. Therefore, what you look like on the inside is far more important than what you look like on the outside.

Consider again our biblical example. What enabled Ruth to catch Boaz's attention? Was it her gorgeous hair or beautiful eyes? No! The answer is found in Boaz's response to her question in Ruth chapter 2.

> *Then she fell on her face, bowing to the ground and said to him, "Why have I found favor in your sight that you should take notice of me, since I am a foreigner?" Boaz replied to her, "All that you have done for your mother-in-law after the death of your husband has been fully reported to me, and how you left your father and mother and the land of your birth, and came to a people that you did not previously know"* (Ruth 2:10-11).

Boaz was attracted to the virtue and character displayed in Ruth's life. Likewise, a man of virtue is irresistible to a godly woman.

An ugly oyster shell is an unlikely place to find a lovely gem, but Isaiah 55:8 says, *"For My thoughts are not your thoughts, nor are your ways My ways...."* You may see an ugly shell, but God sees the beauty He is creating in you. Are the sands of singleness causing you bitterness right now, or are you allowing these trials to change you into a pearl? The Lord wants you to be a Man of Virtue—a pearl of great price (Matt. 13:45-46) for all to admire.

The Gorgeous Body Trap

The world has convinced many Christians that the only way to get a woman's attention is through a gorgeous body. Hollywood has sold the lie that a man will never marry the woman of his dreams if he is not muscular enough or tall enough or handsome! Most dateless men think their condition is the result of the "reflection in the mirror." Consequently, men spend hundreds of hours every year working and pour money into gym memberships believing the myth that a perfectly ripped body is mandatory for marriage.

Proverbs describes how a woman with no character got a man's attention. Some of the descriptives used for her include the following: smooth tongue, captivating eyes, persuasive and seductive speech, a mouth smoother than oil, and flattering speech (see Prov. 5:3; 6:24-25; 7:21). The techniques used today by the modern woman are as old as the first woman who ever snared a man's soul. The whole emphasis is on the superficial, external aspects of a woman—aspects that fade with every passing day. Many women's magazines glorify this woman's techniques rather than expose her bitter end. Marriage based simply on outward beauty can lead to immorality and ultimately, divorce when an even more attractive body comes along.

The Word of God acts as a guide for men in discerning the true value of a woman as a "pearl." Peter warns that a woman's *"beauty should not come from outward adornment, such as braided hair and the wearing of gold jewelry and fine clothes"* (1 Pet. 3:3 NIV). Although braided hair and gold jewelry are not wrong in and of themselves, real beauty is not found on the outside. The key to beauty is found in First Peter 3:4 NIV: *"Instead, it should be that of your inner self, the unfading beauty of a gentle and quiet spirit, which is of great worth in God's sight."* This kind of beauty can only get better the older it gets. As Jackie once said, "If a man chose me for external beauty, his destiny would be hugging a prune. But, if a man chooses me for my internal beauty, his destiny will be unfading beauty even in the twilight years of marriage, because of Jesus."

When you look at the virtuous woman of Proverbs 31:10-31, you will see God's picture of a beautiful woman. There are 20 verses describing her. Only one verse mentions her outward appearance. If a woman were to spend 1/20 of her time on outward physical beauty and the other 19/20 on developing the other qualities God describes as beautiful, such as wisdom, kindness, and godliness, she would become the excellent woman Proverbs 31:10 says a man should try to find.

Remember what King Solomon said in Proverbs 31:30 about the external emphasis of charm and glitz? "Charm is deceptive, and beauty is fleeting; but a woman who fears the Lord is to be praised." There are many women who fear pimples, wrinkles, flabby thighs, and crow's feet, but very few women who really fear the Lord. To which kind of woman are you attracted: the snares of Proverbs 5, 6, and 7, or the beauty of First Peter 3:4?

Fit for a Queen

When you picture the perfect woman for you, what is your princess like? Do you see a woman devoted to God? A woman of character—teachable, loyal, faithful, gentle, and kind? What kind of man do you think this godly woman desires to marry—a shallow man or a man full of charm who knows how to smooth talk and capture other women's attention? Is this the one she imagines she will one day want to spend the rest of her life with—the father of her children? No way!

To marry a princess, you must first become a prince. To marry into royalty, you must be appropriately prepared. A heavenly prince must prepare inwardly for the calling to which he will give his life. As you set your attention on developing godly character, Christ will change you into the handsome prince He created you to be.

Ruth is not the only biblical example of a single person who developed into God's virtuous pearl. Are you becoming a virtuous man that a woman may need as a spouse? Are you using these days to develop godliness in order that, if asked, you will be ready? Whether you marry or not, every man should seek the virtues of Christlikeness.

God desires that men and women develop their inner lives so that through the passing years and fading of outward beauty, their love still deepens and grows. Are you developing into a man who will be able to live "happily ever after"?

To Tell the Truth

There are two ways to get a woman to notice you. The first way, "the gorgeous body trap," is to get her attention by how you look on the outside. This is a snare because looks don't last. They are superficial. The second way is what caused Boaz to notice Ruth and Isaac to be drawn to Rebekah. A Man of Virtue is noticed because he has gained admiration for his godly character. Be truthful. Which approach best represents you? Take the following test. Check the items in each column that describe you most often. Score each total of qualities on the two lists to see if you are developing inner or outer beauty most diligently.

Man of Virtue	**Gorgeous Body**
___ A person to whom all people are attracted (friendly)	___ Nice only to those who can help your dating status

Man of Virtue	**Gorgeous Body**
___ Seeking God first	___ Seeking a relationship first
___ Interesting—with goals for yourself personally	___ "Shopping"— known to be looking for a wife
___ Becoming the man God wants you to be	___ Waiting to be found
___ Realistic	___ Given to self-centered fantasizing
___ Truly interested in the person you date and her best interests	___ Looking for your future in the relationship
___ One who is spiritually challenging	___ Exciting sensuality
___ One who gives friendship	___ One who expects friendship
___ One who communicates verbally	___ Shy
___ Committed to trusting God	___Self-reliant and independent of God
___ Prepared for lasting friendships	___ Playing games
___ Open to other friendships	___ Possessive

Man of Virtue	**Gorgeous Body**
___ Secure in the Lord	___ Insecure without a "dream woman"
___ Building positive qualities	___ Wanting her *now* to yourself
___ Trusting God	___ Trusting in schemes and plans to catch a woman
___ Patiently waiting	___ On the hunt
Score yourself: _____ (total qualities) _____	Score yourself: _____ (total qualities) _____

How did you do? Are you allowing the Holy Spirit to use the sands of singleness to create in you priceless pearls of virtuous character?

Pearl of Character

The pearl-like qualities Ruth and Boaz displayed do not come from the jewelry store; neither are they activated the day she says yes and you place an engagement ring on her finger. Virtue is developed over time as you allow God's Spirit to do a special work in your life.

It is the Holy Spirit, not you, who produces the godly character you seek. These pearls of character are listed in Galatians 5:22-23 as *"... love, joy, peace, patience, kindness, goodness, faithfulness, gentleness, self-control...."* As these qualities develop, your life will reflect the beauty of godly character.

Galatians 5:19-21, however, describes some "fake pearls" with which many singles choose to adorn their lives instead. They are *"...immorality, impurity, sensuality, idolatry, sorcery, enmities, strife, jealousy, outbursts of anger, disputes, dissensions, factions, envying, drunkenness, carousing, and things like these...."* If you desire to be a Man of Virtue, these fake pearls must be removed and replaced with the character quality that pleases God.

How is this done? Confess the sin that developed this unattractive quality. Be honest with yourself and don't cover over or excuse the sin God shows you. Be specific. For instance, instead of saying, "Forgive me for all my many sins," say, "Lord, I have been envious of _____. Forgive me for dwelling on what You have given *him* instead of thanking You for what You have given me." After specifically describing the sin that detracts from your inner beauty, then receive God's forgiveness. His Word says, *"If we confess our sins, He is faithful and righteous to forgive us our sins and to cleanse us from all unrighteousness"* (1 John 1:9). You no longer need to feel condemned or guilty because *"As far as the east is from the west, so far has He removed our transgressions from us"* (Ps. 103:12).

Once you have received God's forgiveness, ask the Lord to cleanse you from whatever caused the sin in the first place. For example, envy often results from comparing yourself to others or from an ungrateful heart. This deeper problem must be changed if envy is to be decisively overcome. If you do not cleanse your heart of these deeper issues, you will find yourself always on your knees asking forgiveness because of a continual struggle with the sin of envy.

One deals with these deeper issues through the power of God's Holy Spirit. He provides the needed power to take care of the deeper issues that produce sinful behavior. Galatians 5:16 speaks of this when it says, *"...walk by the Spirit, and you will not carry out the desire of the flesh."* How does one walk by the Spirit and tap into this pearl-producing power? Three portions of Scripture make it clear.

The first, Ephesians 4:30a, says, *"Do not grieve the Holy Spirit of God."* You grieve or hurt God's Spirit when you choose to think, say, or do something that offends God. To tap into pearl-producing power, you must first decide to live a life that will please your Lord in all respects. From the time you wake in the morning until you go to bed at night, set your heart's desire on exalting Him.

The second verse is found in First Thessalonians 5:19. It says, *"Do not quench the Spirit."* To *quench* gives the word picture of throwing water on a fire. When God's Spirit prompts you to do something, give expression to that impression. Don't douse it with cold water by ignoring His leadership. For example, He may prompt you to perform an act of kindness, or caution you not to say something you are about to say, or lead you to encourage a friend who may be hurting. Whatever it is, seek to obey the Spirit of God in you on a moment-by-moment basis.

Finally, to tap into pearl-producing power, Ephesians 5:18 says, *"...be filled with the Spirit."* To be filled, something must first be empty. To be filled by the Spirit you must be empty of yourself and full of God. You give the Holy Spirit complete and total control of your life. When you became a Christian, you received all of the Holy Spirit. To be a virtuous man, you must let the Holy Spirit have all of you.

There are many imitations of a true pearl, but with years, the shiny pearl paint cracks and wears off and all that is left is an unattractive bead. God's Spirit, however, produces true inner beauty as you confess your sin, avoid displeasing God's Spirit, obey even the slightest of His promptings, and give the Holy Spirit full control of your life. Pearls of godly character take time to develop, which is one reason God calls them "of great price."

You can settle for an imitation pearl by trying to simply cover over ungodly character, or you can allow the Holy Spirit to use the sands of singleness to create the real thing. If you want a cheap imitation, a modeling or charm school will be sufficient for what you seek. But if you want genuine pearls, you must allow the Holy Spirit to perform a special work in your life. Determine to produce pearls of virtue as a treasure for your Lord.

The Pearl
In every oyster there lies the ability
to produce something rare.
Truth like a grain of sand will produce
the pearl that is hidden there...

God makes not mistakes
every life is special,

every life is planned.
Seeds can sprout in sand.

Open yourselves up to the Spirit of God
Grow in grace and maturity
Be what He wants you to be
Your beauty your strength lies deep
within you...

Open yourselves up to God.
Allow Him to reveal your pearl.

Sylvia Hannah

Becoming a Man of Virtue

Read Matthew 7:17-20. How does this passage apply to Samson's life and relationships with women in Judges 13-16? What does it show you about relationships based solely on physical attraction? What character "pearls" (see Gal. 5:22-23) was Samson lacking? Pray about these pearls in your own life. Is God putting His finger on one or more of them?

What books have you read dealing with the virtues/disciplines of a godly man? In contrast, how many magazines or Web pages have you read that deal with external attractiveness? What good books can you begin to read that will help develop your own personal godliness?

_____

_____

_____

_____

Pick out a picture of a man who, according to magazines or the Internet, "has everything." What features do you see? What appeal has been used? What is dangerous about comparing yourself with pictures like that?

_____

_____

_____

_____

Pray, "Father today I choose to cooperate with the Holy Spirit as You make me a Man of Virtue. From my Scripture reading of Galatians 5:16-24, show me one or more qualities that I need to

develop." (For example: discipline, thorough-
ness, graciousness, giving, and diligence.) Pray
over this quality for a month before moving to
something else.

_____

_____

_____

_____

_____

_____

_____

_____

_____

_____

_____

_____

_____

_____

_____

CHAPTER 5

MAN OF DEVOTION

In the receiving line at his younger brother's wedding, many guests greeted Brian over and over with teasing remarks. He heard comments such as, "Always a groomsmen, but never a groom. When is it going to be your turn? The only guy in your family still unmarried!" Though these well-wishers may have been speaking out of fun or even compassion, their speech was not wise. The barrage caused its damage. It is hard enough for a single man to keep his focus where it should be without friends making insensitive comments. How much better it would be for the Right Guy if he was encouraged to pursue his undistracted devotion to the Lord Jesus Christ, instead of being made to feel like he does not quite measure up. If Jesus had been one of the guests, He would have surely commended him for productively using his single time to its fullest.

Much too often, people view a single man as though he should be pitied rather than envied. Nothing could be further from the truth. A single man has the advantage of being able to develop his love relationship with Christ without the distractions that a wife or family inherently brings to one's heart.

This has been God's plan from the beginning. He tenderly created man to love Him and to experience the blessedness of fellowship with Him. In those first days, Adam communed with God in indescribable fellowship and oneness. When God came to walk in the cool of the day, there was no fear, only love. Adam had only positive feelings about God. He loved God, and he knew God loved him. He enjoyed God and devoted himself totally to God's pleasure.

God still desires to know and be known by men today. But because sin entered the world, we no longer have a clear picture of the true God. Satan lied to Eve and—through her—to Adam about God's character. *"Indeed, has God said...?"* (Gen. 3:1). Satan has continued to lie to Eve's children. As a result, fear has often alienated men from the One who loves them as they need to be loved. Deep within a man's soul remains the longing for the embrace of the God Who Is, not the god that the enemy has craftily devised. Consider the cry of the Psalmist, who said, *"My soul faints with longing for your salvation, but I have put my hope in your word"* (Ps. 119:81 NIV).

Boaz spoke of Ruth's devotion to God when he said, *"May the Lord reward your work, and your wages be full from the Lord, the God of Israel, under whose wings you have come to seek refuge"* (Ruth 2:12). Ruth chose to cling to Naomi's God as her own even though her mother-in-law had drawn a negative, harsh picture of Him.

> *She said to them, "Do not call me Naomi* [pleasant]; *call me Mara* [bitter], *for **the Almighty** has dealt very bitterly with me. I went out full, but the Lord has brought me back empty. ...the Lord has witnessed against me and the Almighty has afflicted me?"* (Ruth 1:20-21)

Would you be devoted to a God like Naomi's? In Naomi's bitterness, she no longer referred to God as "the Lord," as she had in verses 8 and 9, but with a title that can cause one to feel alienated and insignificant—"the Almighty." Though Ruth clung to Naomi as a mother, she did not accept her mother-in-law's view of God for herself.

"If we think of Him (God) as cold and exacting, we shall find it impossible to love Him, and our lives will be ridden with servile fear."[1]

Your past experiences, present circumstances, or your parents' devotion or lack thereof may cause you to have an incorrect view of God. But nothing and no one can give you a clearer picture of the true God than slipping under His wings and discovering for yourself who God really is, the refuge and strength for whom you long. He desires for you to come again "into the Garden" and walk with Him in complete fellowship. This is the fullness of devotion.

As a single, you have a wonderful opportunity to use your time to maximize your fellowship with God. When you love someone, you give that person your heart, the center of your being. God asks for no less. He desires a totally devoted heart. Deuteronomy 6:5 says that you are to love Him with all your heart (deepest devotion), your soul (what you think and what you feel), and your might (your strength and energy).

Many men today are devoted, all right! They have devoted themselves to developing a love relationship, but not with the Lord. They erroneously seek for love in sensations and promises. The world's version of love is something they want to "fall into." Meanwhile, "true love" escapes them. True love can only be found in undistracted devotion to Jesus Christ.

To love Him like this, you must know Him intimately. Paul expressed the desire to "know" God in Philippians 3:10. In Greek, this *know* means "a knowledge that perfectly united the subject with the object."[2] Paul was desiring to know God intimately. Second Peter 1:3 says that everything pertaining to life and godliness is yours *"through the true **knowledge** of Him."* Peter and John in Acts 4:13 were identified as uneducated men, but the people observed their confidence and devotion to the Lord and marveled. In the King James Version of Scripture, the people exclaimed that these men *"knew"* Him, or that *"they had been with Jesus."* This "knowing" has the same depth as the term in Genesis 4:1 when Scripture speaks of the intimate relations Adam and Eve had when they *"knew"* or *"had been with"* each other. It is a personal, intimate knowledge. Do you have a devotion to God that causes people to marvel at how intimately you know Him? Do you know God in a way that causes Him to be an intimate, personal part of your being as you may desire a wife to one day be?

As a man, you have been created with a desire to be known—not just in a physical or general way, but deeply known and intimately loved. If you are hoping a woman will one day fill your heart's desire for intimacy, you will be disappointed. God knows your deep longings for intimate love. Only He, the Lover of your soul, can fill this need completely. Your heavenly Father tenderly created you with needs that only God can fully understand and fulfill. As you come to know who He really is, He will meet your needs for love.

Your heavenly Father is incapable of doing evil. He loves you, and forgives and completely forgets confessed sins and grievances. Is this the God you know? If not, you may think you know God, but your responses to God will betray you. If you retract in fear, try to hide things, or give excuses when you do something you feel God would not like, then it shows your knowledge of God, like Naomi's, is incorrect. God is not super-sensitive, selfish, or temperamental.

Do you ever have a feeling of guilt, like you are not doing enough to please God, hanging over your head? Do you feel like the scale of expectations is tipping heavily in the negative and you must balance it? Do you feel like you could never do enough to pay for your inability to be perfect? Then your view of God is incorrect. God is not hard to please. He takes delight in His creation and quickly notices every simple effort to please Him (see Ps. 103:11-14).

Do you feel like God requires too much of you? Do you feel like God denies you the things you need most? If you do, then you don't really know God. Psalm 103:8-14 destroys these wrong assumptions about God. Have you lived with lies about God for too long? Get to know Him.

God wants you to do good and not evil. Jeremiah 29:11 says He wants to give you a future and a hope. Has your wrong picture of God been invented by the enemy in order to rob you of a true knowledge and love of God? Do not be deceived, as Adam and Eve were in the garden. Get to know the One your heart truly desires to love. To love God, you must know Him intimately, personally, and devotedly. This does not require immediate entrance into a convent; you get to know Him by seeking Him.

Seeking True Love

Seeking God is very similar to developing a friendship. You talk a lot, you listen, you write each other letters, you think about each other, you find out what the other likes and does not like, and you try to do things that please that person. The more you spend time together, the more intimately you know your friend. And the more intimately you know your friend, the greater your love will be. It works the same way with your relationship with God.

Jeremiah 29:12-13 promises that a man who diligently seeks God with all his heart will find Him. Your heart is the key to devotion to God. To find God, you must seek Him with your whole heart. A halfhearted search is not sufficient. This means you cannot seek God while you do your own thing.

Is God demanding too much to require that you seek Him with all your heart? No way! Think of it this way: Miss Right comes over one day and begins to speak of her devotion to you. She says what you have been waiting to hear: "I love you. I give you my heart completely. For 364 days of every year, I will devote myself to you and you only." But then she adds, "However, *one* day each year I want to date others and see what I have missed. Don't worry, you can have *all* the rest."

What would your response be? Would you want this kind of devotion? Would it be selfish of you to deny her her heart just one day a year to give to others? No! Absolutely not. You would want her total love and devotion. You would want her heart all 365 days a year. Similarly, giving Christ your heart means you are not free to give it away to other things or people that come into your life (in idolatry). You can't give a part to relationships that delight you in this world and still seek God with a *whole* heart. You cannot keep a part of your heart for something that may seem better if it comes along. Devotion to the Lord Jesus Christ is giving everything or nothing at all. Your devotion to Christ must be a serious commitment to His Lordship. Christ loves you and is completely committed to you. Wholeheartedly devote yourself to loving and enjoying Him in return 365 days a year.

If you are to know God intimately, then you must seek Him, not only with a whole heart, but also with a clean heart. When you think of the word *bride*, you probably first imagine a beautiful, clean, pure woman in white. No grime or dirt mars the image of purity. As a Christian man, you are part of the Bride of Christ. Any grime or dirt of sin will mar your image before Him.

The Lord's fiancé must have a clean heart. You must clean up any blot of sin that may arise between you and your heavenly Lover. Sin causes God to back away from a person. It is disgusting to Him; He will not abide with it. Picture a couple deeply in love. She loves to be near him—so near she can breathe the fresh aroma of his breath! What love! She hates onions though, especially on her beloved's breath. It really turns her off. What do you think he does before he sees her if he has eaten onions? Well, he wouldn't want the sweetness of their fellowship hindered, so he brushes away what offends her. Not only does he brush, but he also "Scopes, Close-ups, and Gleems." He doesn't want to offend his love! He wants nothing to come between them. Sin is far more repulsive to God than even onion breath is to a sweetheart. If you want your devotion to God to be complete, don't merely brush at sin lightly. Get in there and confess it, clean it up, and clear it out. Be rid of it. If you notice you have spiritual halitosis during the day, take care of it immediately. Let Psalm 51:10 be your prayer: *"Create in me a clean heart, O God...."*

Many seek God, but only for His hand. They don't want God as much as they want something from God, such as a woman, happiness, or a family. This impure search for God is limited to what you can get. It is more of a self-love than a God-love. This seeking will end in misery, not in the union of love you desire. God cannot be used like your credit card. He knows your motives. To grow in your knowledge of God, you must seek God correctly, which means you must also seek God with a pure heart.

A man with a pure heart for God does not focus on what He gives, but delights in who He is. He seeks God's *face*, not just His *hand*. Would you want someone to say she loves you just so you would do something for her? To find God, you must seek Him with pure motives. Seek Him for who He is, not just for what He can do for you.

Have you ever tried to develop an intimate relationship with Jana Jabberbox? She's the gal who has lots to say and loves to hear herself say it. You try to say something when she takes a breath—which isn't often—but she keeps right on talking. She never listens. It's a one-way conversation, and you are left out. Even when someone is very special to you, you do not get too excited with a steady monologue. Listening is an important part of developing a closeness with someone else. If you want to get to know the Lord, you must seek Him not only with a whole, clean, and pure heart, but also with a listening heart.

As you spend time with God during your daily devotional time, learn to listen to Him as you read of His love and thoughts about you in the Bible. Think about what He is saying to you personally. Sit silently and write what impressions come to your listening heart. As you read and study His love letters, the Bible, you begin to see what He really thinks of you and what wonderful plans He has for you. As a result, your devotion grows and grows.

To find God you must seek Him with a whole heart, a pure heart, a clean heart, and a listening heart. Hebrews 11:6 NIV says that He *"rewards those who earnestly seek Him."* Does this describe your growing relationship with the Lord?

Singleness does not have to be a curse. Single guys do not have to wear long faces and be pitied until they are finally married. Quite the contrary! Singleness puts you in an advantageous position because, more than likely, you have much more time to seek the Lord now than you will ever have if you marry.

An Advantageous Position

Married men wrestle constantly with having to balance the physical and emotional demands placed on them. All men must learn to balance their priorities, but the single man's heart is not sent in different directions by the needs of a wife and children.

It may be midnight before a husband and father finally gets to an undistracted time for devotion. If he was wise and used his singleness to develop his devotional life, he has resources that allow him to commune with God during the wildest of days. A husband/father who not only works but also helps nurture, guide, and raise his family may find his day beginning early and ending late, often before he has had any uninterrupted time to seek his heart's True Love. A single man can choose to cherish the single time instead of feeling unhappy with it.

The Word of God illustrates the advantageous position of the single man in relation to the affairs of life. *"...An unmarried man is concerned about the Lord's affairs—how he can please the Lord. But a married man is concerned about the affairs of this world—how he can please his wife—and his interests are divided..."* (1 Cor. 7:32-34 NIV).

God says the unmarried man has the advantage when it comes to his devotion to the Lord. An unmarried man can give the Lord what a married man rarely can—undistracted devotion. The time to develop a consistent devotional life cannot wait until you marry. Many single men waste valuable years as they wait "for life to begin"—after marriage. Ask any husband, even without children, and he will tell you his own juggling routine. A married man struggles to have time alone with himself, much less time alone with God.

Becoming the Right Guy, devoted to loving, knowing, and seeking God, will not come cheaply. You are the one who determines the depth of your relationship with God. He does not have favorites. You must choose to pursue the lover of your soul.

A single woman, one who chose to take advantage of her singleness, wrote the following poem:

The Single Gift

How blessed you are, you single one,
Don't talk of care and woes.
You've got too much to be thankful for,
Oh what, you'd like to know.

It's no mistake, no misdirection
Of God's perfect plan
That you've not found your special
  lady
Or you, that certain man.

God loves you so and has much more
To give than you've ever received.
That He's giving His best
  to you right now,
You really must believe.

His best is Himself,
  do you have it in full
Or only a bit on the side.
No man can meet your needs like God,
Nor can a lovely bride.

If your life's not complete, you know
  that Jesus is
And your life He will fill
If you'll only put Him first each day
And live to do His will.

He's gifted you for undistracted
Devotion to the Lord.
There should be nothing that can
  interfere
With Him and prayer and the Word.

Unless you let down the guard of
   your heart
And let others take His place,
Then you'll lack joy and peace and
   hope
And not experience His grace.

So give your heart right back to God,
Let Him keep it safe for you.
And when it's better than His best,
He'll make your one into two.

Donna L. Mihura

God has given you a precious, privileged time. Don't waste a day of it! You will never have it again. These days can be treasure-finding days in your kingly Father's chambers. As you linger at the window ledge searching for a glimmer of Miss Right, don't miss the present precious pearls your Father desires to give to you. Will you grow cold and bitter waiting for your bride, or will you hold your royal head high, glowing in your Father's love and attention? The choice remains with you, strong prince. Your Father will not force you to relinquish your search, but He longs to fellowship with you. Come into His chambers, delight in His Presence. May you be found in Him—a Man of Devotion.

Becoming a Man of Devotion

Read Deuteronomy 30:11-20. What are the benefits of devotion to Christ? What are the results of a life not devoted to Christ?. What gods distract your heart?

_____

_____

_____

List six ways David sought God in Psalm 63. What was his reward?

_____

_____

_____

Are you following hard after Jesus or every eligible girl? Have you come to a place where your relationship with Jesus is beyond comparison with any earthly love? How can you improve your heavenly courtship?

_____

_____

_____

_____

If you have never spent a consistent devotional time with God before now, begin by reading a Psalm a day. After reading the Psalm, write answers to these three questions in a notebook:

_____

_____

_____

What does this passage say about me?

_____

_____

_____

What does this passage say about the Lord?

_____

_____

_____

How can it apply to me?

_____

_____

_____

Endnotes

1. A.W. Tozer, *The Root of the Righteous* (Camp Hill, PA: Christian Publishing, Inc., 1985), 5.
2. W.E. Vine, *Vine's New Testament Dictionary of New Testament Words,* 639.

CHAPTER 6

MAN OF PURITY

No one was surprised when Tim and Susan began dating. They seemed just right for each other. They could talk about anything and had the same ideals for a strong Christian dating relationship. After a year of steady dating, Tim realized how deeply he loved Susan. He began to show his affection for her in different ways. They began to kiss and touch a little. He felt this was all right. He rationalized that he was in control of the situation and intended to remain pure until they married, though neither had ever brought up the subject of marriage.

Their little kisses and touches became more involved, but they always quickly asked forgiveness of each other and God when the petting became intense. After several months of these heavy petting sessions, Tim began to feel distant and uncomfortable.

Gradually, their relationship became more and more physical until one evening, Susan gave Tim the gift she had vowed not to open until her honeymoon night. She had imagined how strong and pure this moment of intimacy would make their love, thinking it would cement the deep love they had for each other. It didn't.

Tim's feelings for Susan changed. They were together, yet further apart than they had ever been. As he rose to leave, he said nothing. Instead of cementing their love, this one act of physical affection destroyed it. Tom longed to take back the treasure of his purity and his relationship with Susan. He wished he could start the night over. Unfortunately, the harsh reality had only just begun.

Tim and Susan are fictitious names, but this is a true story—and not just for this one young man. It is true for hundreds of men who want to do what is right, but who unwisely give away their gift of physical purity too early. The gift is a treasure that can be rewrapped and given again, but never again for the first time.

We live in a day of blatant sexual impurity. A man who marries, still a virgin, has become the exception, not the rule. Statistics say 80 percent of all unmarried men have given away their virginity by 20 years of age.[1] The Ruth and Boaz of our biblical story, like us, also lived in a society of rampant moral decay. Their story occurs during a time of year when sexual promiscuity would be at its height in the small farming community of Israel. "Immoral practices at harvest times were by no means uncommon and, indeed appear to have been encouraged by the fertility rites practiced in some religions."[2]

In this promiscuous society Ruth and Boaz were people of purity, even in the midst of a potentially compromising situation. Ruth 3:7 says, *"When Boaz had eaten and drunk and his heart was merry, he went to lie down at the end of the heap of grain; and she came secretly, and uncovered his feet and lay down."* At a glance, you may read this and picture the beginnings of an X-rated scene in Ruth's story. But you must realize that Ruth was acting according to the customs of the time. She was not slinking into Boaz's bed to seduce him. In obedience to her mother-in-law's instructions, Ruth quietly lay at his feet for him to notice her, thus symbolizing her subjection to Boaz as her nearest of kin. This would give him the opportunity, if he so chose, to take legal action for the well-being of Ruth and her mother-in-law. (A woman had no form of social security and very few rights in that culture without a man.) This was not a brazen act of seduction, but an act of obedience to God's plan for her provision in that day. One thing is certain. When she left to go home, she walked away as a person of purity, and the whole time she was with Boaz, he treated her as a woman of virtue and protected her honor:

> And now, my daughter, don't be afraid. I will do for you all you ask. All my fellow townsmen know that you are a woman of noble character. Although it is true that I am near of kin, there is a kinsman-redeemer nearer than I. Stay here for the night, and in the morning if he wants to redeem, good; let him redeem. But if he is not willing, as surely as the Lord lives, I will do it. Lie here until morning. So she lay at his feet until morning, but got up before anyone could be recognized; and he said, "Don't let it be known that a woman came to the threshing floor....Then she told [Naomi] everything Boaz had done for her and added, "He gave me these six measures of barley, saying,

> *"Don't go back to your bother-in-law empty-handed." Then Naomi said, "Wait, my daughter, until you find out what happens. For the man will not rest until the matter is settled today"* (Ruth 3:11-18 NIV).

Although the customs of Ruth's day may be difficult to understand, the temptations to compromise physically are not. Unfortunately, many men have been snared by the devil's deceptions and robbed of their innocence. How does today's single man safeguard this special treasure and, like Boaz and Ruth, go home at night a person of purity?

Deadly Deception

Remember how the serpent deceived Eve by causing her to question God? He caused her to believe that God wanted to deny her something good, not provide her with something better. The enemy wants you to believe that if you wait to have sex, you will miss out on some of the delights of life.

Godly men must avoid basing their comprehension of the pleasures of sex on what commercials advertise, magazines and the Internet glamorize, or books and movies sensationalize. These are all full of the enemy's propaganda. Today's society seeks ultimate pleasure with no pain. But following society's example usually brings just the opposite. Look to your heavenly Father, your Creator, for the truth. God gives true sexual fulfillment to the man who waits for this gift. God intended for you to enjoy the fulfillment and pleasure of sex within marriage only. The wonder and joy of this intimate act is maximized through purity before marriage.

Ask any man of God who waited, and he will tell you that it was worth the sacrifice of denying his desires for a time. Look at that man's marriage. Most likely, the romance between him and his spouse still burns in a delightful love affair. Compare this real-life situation to the illusions of sex portrayed in movies. Have those actors and actresses (who, by the way, never scrub a toilet, go bald, or work on tax forms) found true fulfillment? According to the movie scripts, they should. "Ah! Yes—the delights of sex." Do not be deceived. Sex is special! Sex with the bride God created for you is satisfying sex in your Creator's way and time.

Why Wait?

Since sex is desirable, why not have sex? Why would God want to limit your pleasure with someone for whom you feel affection, but haven't married? Have you ever been dieting, but treated yourself to a huge piece of rich chocolate cake with fudge icing to celebrate some special occasion? Cake is good. Cake is desirable. The more cake, the more pleasure. But cake, in the midst of a strict diet, can really make one sick! The pleasure of a big, luscious piece of cake depends on the right timing, just as the pleasures of sex do.

God wants you to be a Man of Purity because He wants to protect you from the consequences that sex before marriage brings. These consequences can be physical, emotional, relational, and spiritual. Let's look at these a little more closely.

Physical

Have you ever secretly opened a Christmas gift before Christmas Day and rewrapped it, putting it back under the tree? How thrilling and exciting it was when you saw the surprise. But what about the "big day," when the gifts were supposed to be opened for the first time? Where was the excitement when you opened your gift? The gift did not seem quite as special because it had already been opened for the first time. Each man receives one "first time." God desires for your valuable gift to be given to a committed lover who will cherish, keep, and protect you in marriage. God wants you and your gift to this woman to be treasured and cherished, not trampled or depreciated. Song of Solomon 8:4 NIV says, "...*Do not arouse or awaken love until it so desires.*" God wants to protect you from losing your virginity— or to forgive and cleanse you from past sins of impurity and set you on a fresh course as a new man.

God also wants to protect you from the sexually transmitted diseases that could affect not only you but also your future wife. One young single cried the night he discovered that he had contracted genital warts. He grieved over the realization that when his future princess arrived, before he could propose, he would have to disclose the fact that he carried an infectious disease. This grieved him more than the fact that genital warts are incurable. Not only could you or your wife personally incur irreparable physical damage, but also transmit these infectious diseases to your future children.

God also desires to shield you from an un-
wanted pregnancy. Although precautions exist,
pregnancy always remains a possibility. A rushed
marriage, adoption, or abortion only complicate
the consequences.

Devon had graduated from high school and
was preparing to enter Christian college to become a minister. On his finger was a promise
ring—a commitment to remain pure until marriage. But one night of passion made him forget
the ring, and nine months later, he was a father,
ejected from the college on a morals clause. Regardless of how sorry he was and the fact that
God had forgiven him, the consequences of that
one act changed his life forever. For years, Devon
struggled with how God could have allowed that
one mistake to ruin his life, and in his anger, he
ran from God. God wanted to protect Devon, but
He left the choices up to him. Mercifully, our God
is a God of forgiveness and healing—Manasseh
and Ephraim. Zechariah 1:3 NIV says, *"Return
to me,' declares the Lord Almighty, 'and I will return to you.'"*

Devon returned to God, and God brought
healing to the relationship with his child's mother.
They found love in Christ, and now are married
with more children. It wasn't according to God's

perfect plan, but God can take even disasters and make something beautiful, if His people will call on His name.

God desires to shield you from the negative physical consequences of premarital sex. He wants to protect you from sinning against your body. First Corinthians 6:18 NIV says, *"Flee from sexual immorality. All other sins a man commits are outside his body, but he who sins sexually sins against his own body."* "He wants you to be free from an addiction to premarital sex. Passionate physical exchange is a short-lived high. As with drugs, you keep wanting more intense highs."[3]

God wants to protect you from the devastation of condemnation. The devil loves to get you down, to make you feel unworthy, thus making you unable to glorify God or stand before others. He enhances this tactic when he can whisper in your ear, "Some Christian you are. How can you witness to Jason? He probably heard what a hypocrite you are.... You can't be a missionary; you compromised, remember? You are condemned... condemned...condemned."

If you gave away your treasure to the wrong woman, haunting fears may also begin to plague you. "Will she still respect me? Will she still love me? What if she's pregnant? Will anyone else find out? What if my parents find out? How can I face them? If we break up, what if the next woman I date finds out?" Day and night these fears can play on your mind and emotions. God wants to protect you from these emotional traumas.

After premarital sex, there will usually be some lurking doubts. Would she have loved me without my body? Would she have married me if she hadn't gotten pregnant? Most overwhelming are the doubts of God's love for you and, possibly, doubts of your salvation or your ability to ever again have a morally pure relationship.

You can be fully forgiven and cleansed by Christ, but damaged emotions take time to heal. The Lord doesn't want you to suffer these hurts. You are precious to Him. That's why He sets loving limits on your physical relationships and emotional attachments.

The emotional burdens of condemnation, fear, and doubt are often compounded with many other emotions such as resentment, bitterness, depression, and mistrust. God created you with emotions that can be overwhelmed by sexual promiscuity. Let Him protect your heart.

Relational

A man has a depth of soul that desires an intimate friendship, apart from anything physical, with the woman he loves. He desires to be known and respected for the man he is, not just for his physical body. A couple who chooses to remain physically pure gives all their time and attention to knowing one another on a deeper mental and emotional level. Once passion is introduced into the relationship, it is difficult to stop and be satisfied again with just developing the friendship. The man becomes distracted by the physical. Something is lost when physical passion begins.

You cannot give double messages. Either you want her to know the you on the inside or the you on the outside. If you encourage your date to play with the bow on your package, she will want to untie the ribbon and unwrap the gift. Don't distract her with the bow. As a man of God, protect your relationships with women by treating them as sisters (1 Tim. 5:2) and not allowing sex to enter into a relationship before marriage.

Premarital sex also brings a consequence that remains hidden until you marry. Mistrust and disrespect surface after the wedding cake has been eaten and "post-marital insecurity" begins. When a couple becomes involved sexually before marriage, they massage their consciences with the rationalization that they will marry anyway, so their lack of self-control doesn't matter. This is where they are wrong! Lack of self-control before marriage is *fornication*. Lack of self-control after marriage is *adultery*. The seeds for adultery are planted in the "hotbeds" of fornication. Your wife will subconsciously wonder, "If he did not exhibit self-control with me before marriage, how can I be sure that he will not give in to temptation during marriage when a more attractive woman comes along?" A young man who cannot control himself before marriage does not suddenly become a man of self-control because he wears a wedding band!

Two other very real relational consequences deal with your present and future families. Think of your parents' shame about your sexual choices. Also, what about your future children? One day, you may face your children's knowing that you did not set an example of purity for them to follow. What will you say if they ask the question, "Did you and Mom wait?"

Finally, should you not marry the woman who opened your gift first, you take memories of her into your marriage that flash back to haunt you. God wants you to have the joy of saying to your princess on that special wedding night, "Here I am, clean and pure, emotionally and physically. No one has touched the treasure of my love. I kept myself for you."

God knows that a man has much more to offer than a body. He knows that the dynamic relationship a man has with a woman is more than a physical experience. God intended for man and woman to enjoy not merely sexual intercourse, but a love that the physical relationship merely enhances. This love remains even when there is no physical culmination. Sometimes physical contact distracts a couple from developing and enjoying communication. If you want the friendship to be knowing who you each are, don't distract each other with early or inappropriate physical contact.

Spiritual

Passion makes it difficult to see that God also set physical limits to protect you spiritually. Hebrews 13:4 NIV very clearly says that *"Marriage should be honored by all, and the marriage bed kept pure, for God will judge the adulterer and all the sexually immoral."* God judges the sin of immorality. It feels awful to be separated from your Lord by the guilt of sin.

Actions speak louder than words, and this is especially true regarding premarital sex. It is difficult to share Christ with one who knows your reputation. Your actions can also cause weaker brothers and sisters to stumble. One night of passion can totally destroy a reputation you have built over a lifetime.

The spiritual side of sex is often overlooked. Even many Christians are not aware of the profoundly spiritual nature of their sex lives. A person will feel acute spiritual pain and separation from God when engaging in sex outside of marriage, but may not even realize how spiritually beneficial and unifying sex is within marriage.[4]

God does not intend to deny you pleasure. He protects you so you might enjoy physical health, emotional stability, relational intimacy, and spiritual blessings. If you marry, He wants you to grow more in love with your wife with each passing year. He wants you to live in complete trust of one another and spend a lifetime in love instead of the consequences of a fleeting night of uncontrolled lust.

Guarding the Treasure

How, then, does the Right Guy guard his purity? Once a woman has a man's heart, his body is not far behind. That is one reason Proverbs 4:23 says, *"Watch over your heart with all diligence, for from it flow the springs of life."* To walk in purity, the Right Guy must first guard the key to his heart. This does not imply that your relationships with women are robotic and free from feelings. It means that you focus on growing in friendship, not romance.

They had known each other a month when Brandon surprised her by saying, "I love you." Kara hadn't even thought about love yet. What did he mean? What did he *want?* She liked him; she thought she respected him, but she wasn't sure if she knew him well enough to love him. She felt pressured to make a decision, then. Before, it had been going so well, but now, she had to decide: Do I love him, too? If I do, what does that mean? If I don't, is it over? Brandon had found Miss Right and had intended to move slower—to enjoy their growing relationship. But in one moment, he had scared her, and it was several weeks before he was able to return to that place where they had been so comfortable in getting to know each other.

Don't let your heart be given away too easily. "I love you" has a lot of meanings, depending on the context and the audience. If a woman says she loves you, you don't have to echo the phrase. To men, these words can mean all kinds of things, like "I lust for you," or "I want you to kiss me." Or maybe he just can't think of anything else to say at the moment! To women, it might mean you make me feel happy and safe—like a brother...like a friend...like a fellow child of Christ. She might even throw in a hug. But what did that "I love you" do to your heartstrings? Gradually, those "I love yous" can trap you emotionally and lead you on physically. To guard the key to your heart, make a commitment to say you love someone only if you love her with a committed love, not a casual love feeling. You will remain much more in control of your friendship. Real love will have time to blossom and grow without those three words. Guard and save them to be whispered when God reveals it is time. What a gift to tell that special woman as you propose, "You are the first person I have ever said this to: 'I love you.'" Give meaning to those precious words, and you may use them and hear them with fondness through many happy years of marriage.

There's a second step you can take to guard your purity. It's a radical statement, but save all your kisses for your future wife.

A man's kiss or embrace is not just another way of saying thank you! A kiss should say something more intimate. If so, do you want to say intimate things to every girl you date? All the kisses you give before marriage and all the kisses you give after marriage express the love that belongs to one person: your princess.

If you remember to whom your kisses belong, you won't be so quick to give them away. If you think you may be dating Miss Right, give your friendship time to grow before you initiate the "fringe benefits." She will appreciate them and respect you much more if you wait.

Realize that a kiss starts physical contact, and once you get started, it's hard to turn back from passion. Determine what you mean with a kiss. Let it reveal your heart, not "rev up" your hormones. One person put it this way when asked why "friends" have trouble becoming friends again once they start dating: "Once you start having sex, that's about the only thing you have in common."

A third practical step is to make your decisions and choices about what you will and will not do with a date *before* things become hot and heavy. Here are some examples of "dating standards" that many godly men have made. They will help you resist the pressure to "open the gift" too early. (You can find more in Chapter 9.)

- I will date only growing Christian women. (You will most likely marry a woman you date. This is important!!)

- I will concentrate on the friendship—not romance. (Don't be tricked!)

- I will not spend time with her at home when we are alone.

- I will not give kisses and hugs freely.

- I will not lay down beside a woman.

Don't set standards "as you go." Emotions can be tricky. You must make wise choices before the "flutters" and "heartthrobs" become so loud you cannot hear yourself think. Write them down and read them often! Commit them to God regularly in prayer.

During a Bible study, one single made this point about "dating."

> Before Jesus became Lord of my relationships, I accepted our society's idea of dating as the time for a man and woman to be alone together. This time usually was devoted to romance and involved a measure of physical involvement—gradually accelerating if the dating continued. As I became closer to the Lord, I began to see dating from His perspective as a time for friendship-building without a need for promises of love or giving physical affection. As I spend time in group situations instead of one-to-one dating, I can really see the character of the ...friends I am spending time with. Doing things with groups also guards our purity, but doesn't limit our friendship-building and communication. ...I don't refer to it as dating any longer. I talk about 'friendship-building' founded on Christ—the One who holds my heart and guides the friendship.

Where Are the Modern Bravehearts?

Our society is in deep need of bravehearted men protecting women rather than exploiting them. Boaz's said in Ruth 2:9 NIV... *"I have told the men not to touch you."* Where are the modern Bravehearts?

> To have the Spirit of God dwelling within the heart of someone who chooses a domesticated faith is like having a tiger trapped within a cage. You are not intended to be a spiritual zoo where people can look at God in you from a safe distance. You are a jungle where the Spirit roams wild and free in your life. You are the recipient of the God who cannot be tamed and a faith that must not be tamed. You are no longer a prisoner of time and space, but a citizen of the kingdom of God—a resident of the barbarian tribe. God is not a sedative that keeps you calm and under control by dulling your senses. He does quite the opposite. He awakens your spirit to be truly alive.[5]

Purity When Alone

Pornography and Butterflies

Here is a rough summation of a sobering story concerning the impact of pornography on a man's sexual life:

During the mating season for butterflies, a group of male and female butterflies were placed in a controlled-environment cage. In the center of the cage was an artificial copy of the most beautiful female butterfly. The female butterfly mannequin had extra high-gloss coloring making her superior to any real female butterfly. When the scientists released the male and female butterflies into the cage, the males immediately tried to mate with the high-gloss mannequin. The test team watched as the male butterflies kept slamming up against the fake butterfly, persisting in their attempts to mate. Consequently, the male butterflies beat themselves to death up against the fake mannequin, leaving no male butterflies with the capacity to mate with real butterflies.

If this story seems absolutely far-fetched to your heart and soul, it would greatly benefit you to do some research concerning the impact of pornography on the men in our society. You can read books like *Every Man's Battle* or you can log on the Internet and read some articles by Patsy Rae Dawson on *Adultery and Sexual Addiction*.[6]

What If It's Too Late?

You do not have to make the same mistakes many have made. But if you are reading this "after the fact" and are dealing with the guilt of the lost gift, do not be discouraged. Although it is true that there is only one first time, God is the God of the first-time experience. Let Him heal your broken heart through forgiveness. Agree with God that you have sinned and leave the sin before Him. Then guard yourself from entering into that sin pattern again. Learn a valuable lesson, but do not continue to beat yourself with condemnation. Jesus paid for those sins at Calvary. Do not continue to allow yourself or the enemy to defeat you with remembering a sin once you have confessed it to God and those you have offended. There may be consequences of your sin, but you do not have to live with the guilt of it.

God is the God who forgives and forgets. Jeremiah 31:34 says, *"...for I will forgive their iniquity, and their sin I will remember no more."* One of God's greatest abilities is that He forgets the sins of those who belong to Christ Jesus, *"I, even I, am the One who wipes out your transgressions for My own sake; and I will not remember your sins"* (Isa. 43:25). Let this be your motto: *"...but one thing I do: forgetting what lies behind* [as God does] *and reaching forward to what lies ahead, I press on toward the goal for the prize of the upward call of God in Christ Jesus"* (Phil. 3:13-14).

Even though you have been freed from the guilt by confession, do not use it as an opportunity to continue in sin or to leave yourself open to temptation. Continue to choose freedom over sin's mastery. Lay aside every encumbrance and the sin that so easily entangles you and run with endurance the race set before you (see Heb. 12:1). How? Fix your eyes on Jesus (not on your sin, the past, or even yourself). Jesus is the author and perfector of your faith (see Heb. 12:2).

There is one last response that brings complete freedom. You must forgive and forget the sins of those who sinned against you. Jesus is very clear in Matthew 5:21-24 about what to do with anger toward another. But how do you do it? First, choose to forgive the person with your heart and then God will help you work through the emotions that may remain. You will not be free of the hurt if you harbor bitterness. A quick way to ruin a great complexion is to hold on to an unforgiving, bitter attitude.

If you have opened your gift too soon, do not be kept from beginning new again. Accept God's forgiveness and refuse to feel like damaged goods. God has better in store for you. You, Right Guy, are a treasure. The enemy attempts to deceive you when he offers to delight you by his ways and means. Don't lose sight of the value of what you have or of who you are. Don't allow the flickering pleasures of an evening of "making love" destroy a lifetime of "lasting love."

Becoming a Man of Purity

Second Samuel 13:1-19 is a painful story of rape, but note the reaction of the man who got what he wanted. After his sexual thirst was quenched, what was his response toward the woman for whom he lusted? How did he feel toward the woman? Why?

_____

_____

_____

_____

How can a young man stay pure? (See Psalm 119:9,11 and Romans 8:3-8.) Is striving to be pure too hard? Read First Corinthians 10:13 and list some of the ways of escape God has given you.

_____

_____

_____

How do friendships affect your purity? (See First Corinthians 15:33.)

_____

_____

_____

Write out a specific list of ways you will guard your purity as you build relationships with the opposite sex. Include a discussion of what you are trying to communicate to a woman by kissing her. Is there any other way to say this?

_____

_____

_____

_____

Endnotes

1. Nadine Joseph, "The New Rules of Courtship," *Newsweek Magazine*, Special Edition, Summer/Fall (1990), 27.
2. Arthur E. Cundall and Leon Morris, *Judges and Ruth, an Introduction and Commentary* (Downers Grove, IL: InterVarsity Press, 1968), 287.
3. Tim Stanford, "The Best of Sex," *Campus Life Magazine*, February (1992), 25–26.
4. Ibid., 25–26.
5. Erwin R. McManus, *The Barbarian Way* (Nashville: Nelson Books, 2005), 66.
6. See Stephen Arterburn, *Every Man's Battle* (Colorado Springs: WaterBrook Press, 2000); and Patsy Rae Dawson, *Adultery and Sexual Addiction* (Amarillo, TX: Gospel Themes Press, 1998), http://gospelthemes.com/asa.htm.

CHAPTER 7

MAN OF SECURITY

What does an ideal Christian man look like in the twenty-first century?

Courage

An ideal Christian man in the twenty-first century is one that is marked by courage. A man cannot aspire to anything if he does not start with courage. Courage is the platform we begin from because of the fierce task that lies before any man who decides to lay down his life in a world that calls him to fight for everything he can get his hands on. This might seem to be a contradiction, since most people associate courage with fighting. In some cases this is true, but a man is also called to a courage that involves not physical fighting, but ultimate dying.

It takes a lot of courage to die, and that is what we are called to do as Christians (see Luke 9:23-24). If a man wants to truly follow Christ, he must die to himself. He must die to his instinct to secure his future and hoard his possessions. He must not trust in his own abilities or his own cleverness to get what he wants. He must put others before himself even if it takes his time, energy, or even finances.

It takes courage to give someone in need the last five-dollar bill in your pocket to get some food instead of feeding yourself. It takes courage to spend your time sitting with a friend who just lost a parent. It takes courage to invest your energy in a "lost cause" (whether a person or a project), without any promise of return, but these are the exact things the Lord has done for us. Besides, if we are ever going to see God move, it will only be if we had the courage to open up the opportunities for Him to show himself.

Sacrifice

Sacrificing is a natural transition when speaking about dying to oneself in the way

Christ died for us. Sacrificing is not often talked about outside of sports. In baseball, you hear about a sacrifice fly, or someone sacrificing his body to make a play. No matter how the term is used, sacrificing almost always means putting oneself aside for the good of the team or the end goal.

The sacrificing we are called to as men of Christ is similar to the sacrificing necessary in sports. We are supposed to be men who put aside our own desires, our own welfare, and our own gain for the good of the team. There will be many times in our lives when we will be called to sacrifice as men of God. Maybe you will have to sacrifice your reputation as "the cool guy" to hang out with someone who doesn't seem to have as many friends as you. Maybe you will have to sacrifice your own pleasure for the moment in order to keep your integrity for a lifetime. Maybe you will have to sacrifice pleasing everyone (which is never possible) in order to serve the one you know who needs it.

We are men who are taught in the Bible to live by faith and not by sight, but our culture is so "visible." Our culture teaches us that if we can see it, then it is real. If we can touch it, then it can be ours with just enough hard work and effort. If we can put our hands on it, then we can own it. But we are meant to live for the unseen, for the eternal, and for that which can be stored up in heaven and not simply on earth. When we realize the difference between what the world lives for as compared to what we as Christians live for, we will see the sacrifices we need to make.

Trust

It is impossible to read through the Bible and not see men trusting God. The "Hall of Faith" in Hebrews 11 records men of the past who trusted in God for something they could not provide themselves. The psalms of King David are infused with this same trust, no matter what the circumstances, no matter who the enemy.

Somehow, we have missed this point as men today. We have grown up in a culture that offers the hope of the American dream and promotes the self-made man. We can name plenty of stories of men who have started from humble beginnings and now sit on executive boards as entrepreneurs and CEOs. Their strategies, however, are often much different from God's.

Contrary to popular belief, nowhere in the Bible does it say, "God helps those who help themselves." However, the Bible does say, *"For everyone who exalts himself will be humbled, and he who humbles himself will be exalted"* (Luke 14:11). To make oneself low in the eyes of the world shows a lot of trust in God. It takes a lot of trust to be honest on your taxes, knowing God will provide, instead of being conniving and deceptive and using your own wits to finagle the numbers for certain gain. It takes a lot of trust to leave your children in the hands of the Lord and promote their God-given gifts instead of cramming them into the mold of the next successful doctor or lawyer you want them to be. It takes a lot of trust to quit your job because you feel your duties in your company compromise your integrity.

It is exactly this kind of trust that the Lord delights in, and it is exactly this kind of trust that brings life to a man's soul. To trust the Lord, to take risks for the sake of His name and your integrity, is an adventure. If you are bored (which it is said of many men in our churches are today), then step out and trust the Lord. He promises to give you all the adventure and breath-taking risks you can handle.

Self-awareness

This concept might initially sound like a New Age philosophy, but it is actually very realistic and even biblical. When David asked the Lord to search his heart and find any offensive way in him in Psalm 51, he was asking the Lord to know himself in order that he may know God. As men in the twenty-first century, we have become very good at masking who we are. We have been told we are to be the strong ones, the providers, and the rocks of our families, businesses, and friendships. However, so often we are trying to maintain our façade of stability while ignoring the shaky ground that is the "bedrock" of our souls.

So you might be thinking, "OK, so what if I look down in the depths of my soul? Do you just want me to get in touch with my feminine side?" No. We need to be in touch with our depravity so we may know the extent of His mercy. C.S. Lewis puts it this way: "A recovery of the old sense of sin is essential to Christianity. Christ takes it for granted that men are bad. Until we really feel this assumption of His to be true, though we are part of the world He came to save, we are not part of the audience to whom His words are addressed."[1]

I don't want to miss out on what Jesus has to offer, and I don't want you to, either.

In order for us to not miss out on what Jesus was offering, we will have to see the sin in our own lives and the grace He offers us by removing it. If we never see our own sin, then we will never see Him remove anything—and then what is Christianity for us? Mere principles to live by in order for us to appear "good" to everyone else? If we do not see the depth of our depravity, then we will never see the height of His mercy.

For instance, how grateful are we when we are given something we deserve as compared to something we do not deserve yet are given anyway? No one wants to be handed the first place trophy before the beginning of the season. What feels so good about receiving that trophy is knowing you put in the hard work and long hours to earn it. This usually leaves us with a distorted sense of self, being self-sufficient and prideful.

However, let's say when you turned 16, you didn't have enough money to buy a car. Knowing this, your grandfather decides to give you his pick-up truck without you even as much as asking him for it—and not just an old junker, but a sharp-looking 4×4. You would be so grateful for his gift because he didn't have to give it to you. You hadn't done anything to merit that car. You didn't earn it at all. In fact, you would probably be very humbled to receive a gift of that magnitude. You see, if we don't deserve it, we are more thankful for it. This is how it is with God's grace. We do not deserve it, yet it is given to us, despite the things that lie deep within our "*wicked and deceitful*" hearts (Jer. 17:9).

It is only once we "remember the height from which we have fallen" that we can live as men who are marked by grace, mercy, and thankfulness. If we are only men who believe you receive what you have earned, then we will be men who are very legalistic and probably very judgmental toward our friends, co-workers, and families. But, if we look into our own hearts, see the depravity, sin, and selfishness that is within ourselves, we will be thankful to God as we see him delivering us from these habits that we are no longer enslaved to. We will also be more forgiving toward people in whom we see those same things.

To look at one's soul barren, fragile, and broken, takes a lot of courage and trust (the qualities mentioned before). We must have the courage to see ourselves for who we really are, not simply the mask we put on (by identifying ourselves simply by what we do, where we live, or what degrees we hold). When we look at ourselves this way, we may want to go back to the naivety we previously held, but this is not an option. We may think, "If I stop looking at the sin in my own heart, I can forget about it and it will go away," but it won't. Only God can take it away, and he wants to.

This is why we must trust him as the author and perfector of our faith, *"being confident of this, that he who began a good work in you will carry it on to completion until the day of Christ Jesus"* (Phil. 1:6 NIV). We must trust him that no sin is too big for him to wash away. His love and forgiveness is greater than our mistakes, but we cannot experience those great things He offers unless we venture into the untouched and unseen parts of our soul.

Don't be fooled, though—this will be painful, just as the most sensitive parts on your bodies are the ones unseen. You don't mind someone poking you on the arm, but as soon as they poke you in your armpit, you get annoyed. The places of your soul that have not been touched will naturally be sensitive when examined, but remember, those are the places of most importance, just as the most important things of your body are the things that no one can see, such as your heart and lungs.

It is not only depravity we will see as we plunge into the deepest parts of our souls. We will also see the very fabric by which we were made. We will begin to see how the Lord has gifted us, which will then lead to our service for him. The Lord has gifted his people with all kinds of gifts, some of which are things that we do and some of which are not simply actions at all. Each gift, however, is not simply what we are told we are good at doing.

Gifts can be activities in which we excel, or even convictions on which we are firm. If I enjoy meeting new people and making them feel welcome at parties or gatherings, maybe that is my gift. Or maybe I am really good at fixing people's cars. This could be my gift, as well. Gifts can be so many things, as long as they are given *"for the least of these"* (Matt. 25:40). However, if we do not take a hard look at ourselves in the mirror, these things that lurk beneath may never surface, and therefore may never be utilized. This will leave us feeling unfulfilled or inadequate because we are trying to squeeze ourselves into this little box the world is telling us we must, should, and do fit into.

Community

"No man is an island," and neither is any Christian. As Christians, we were made for each other. It was not good for us to be alone; therefore, we are helpers to each other. We all have different needs and abilities, so we all fit together to make one functioning unit. We are not meant to carry out burdens alone, but to cast them upon the Lord, and to confess our sins to one another. (See 1 Peter 5:17 and James 5:16.) If you thought you were meant to be a Lone Ranger, you are sadly mistaken.

There is a community life of the Christian—one of fellowship, sharpening, and serving—that each of us must be a part of. We must be willing to rub up against one another if we are ever going to be changed into the people God wants us to be. For instance, did you know that a washing machine gets clothes clean because the clothes rub up against each other? (College guys, this is why you are not supposed to pack the washer so full that you have to sit on top of it just to get it to start—the clothes have to have room to move around!) Clothes become clean with a little bit of soap and a lot of rubbing against each other.

The Lord has put us in this washing machine called the world and given us the one thing that can make us clean, called the Holy Spirit. It is only when we interact with each other with the Holy Spirit being a part of our lives that any sort of cleanliness can occur. Sometimes we get rubbed the wrong way by people and we feel that they are rude or inconsiderate, but that only reveals how dirty we are and how clean we need to become.

Honorable

Jesse had picked a strong girl, someone who could stand on her own two feet. She would have a career, he would have a career, and they would be sitting pretty, financially. If the relationship was a little, well, robotic—hey, you can't have everything. She was pretty, smart, and loved Christ. She looked good on paper, and that's what he wanted. He checked "find a wife" off the list and planned to propose—sometime before college graduation, probably. But then, her car broke down, and she called him to rescue her. It was an inconvenient time, and she was a strong woman, right? So he told her to call a tow truck, and he'd see her on the weekend. He was shocked when she called her brother-in-law instead and broke up with him that weekend.

Men, God has made you princes in His kingdom. Your job is not to go searching for a damsel in distress. In fact, a damsel *constantly* in distress might be a warning sign that her focus and maturity are not where they need to be. But if God places a woman under your care and she is in distress—you had better come to her aid. Christ gave His life for His Bride; the least we can do is change a flat tire for the woman we are dating (see Eph. 5:25).

Obedient

You are not your own master, and until you realize it, you are in for a frustrating life. Men of God are meant to be obedient men of God. We are men who have been bought with a price... and know it. We are men who understand "costly grace," as opposed to "cheap grace," as described by Dietrich Bonhoeffer.[2] Bonhoeffer knew that men could not be recipients of something so great as eternal life and pardon from damnation, without receiving a responsibility as well. As recipients of grace, you now have a responsibility—or, an even better way to look at it, a privilege—to serve your master, who is God.

Unfortunately, many people use this grace to serve themselves. You might be asking, "When have you seen someone deliberately take the grace of God and use it to serve themselves?" I say to you, my friend—every day. God's grace shines on us all, because none of us deserve it. We are all given life, breath, strength, and energy every day, but there are still plenty of people who do not use those gifts to serve God. To serve yourself every day would mean that you have accepted "cheap grace." However, to understand the grace that you have been given and, in turn, to be so grateful that you want to give it all back in praise, service, and admiration to the giver because you understand the price he paid to give it to you, now that is "costly grace."

But do not be afraid. After realizing where you are, and where you have come from by God's grace, you do not have to be a missionary to a small, unreached people group—unless this is where God calls you. However, this is admirable and may be within your gifts, abilities, and opportunities. All God asks you to do is something very simple: Be faithful with the little—and, in this I mean, be obedient to God in the everyday things.

You don't have to be the next Billy Graham. You don't have to be the next super-preacher or super-missionary. You just need to be who God created you to be with all your wonderful gifts and abilities that are dependent upon Him, and live for Him wherever you are. If He wants you to go to the mission field, He'll let you know, and He'll equip you for the journey.

If the Lord has placed you around three friends at the moment, be obedient by loving, encouraging, and supporting them as best as possible. Maybe you feel like you are just a working man. If you are, then have integrity in the things you do at work. Or maybe if you are in school, you need to honor the Lord in the way you study. Whatever it is, and wherever you are, be a man who serves God and his people. You do not need a specific "calling" or "vision" to do anything like that. All you need to do is spend time learning about how Jesus did that every day and then do what He did in your own world. If every man did that, we would not need "missionaries" because we would all be missionaries; no one would need to be "called into ministry," because we would *all* be doing ministry. If every man lived like that, then we would be the men God wanted us to be who loved him and his people.

Becoming a Man of Security

Consider the things that are most important to you. What do you spend your most energy and time on? If these were taken away, how would you be affected?

_____

_____

_____

Meditate on Colossians 3:1-3. True security is basing your life on that which cannot be taken away. Where should your focus be?

_____

_____

_____

Read Hebrews 13:4-5. How would having your security in the Lord and not in the woman you are dating affect how you might react if the dating relationship ended?

_____

_____

_____

_____

Meditate on Ephesians 5:25-33. Make a list of characteristics of an honorable man. How does this list of characteristics help you feel more secure in your relationship to Christ and any woman you might date?

_____

_____

_____

_____

_____

_____

_____

_____

_____

_____

Endnotes

1. Gerard Reed, *C.S. Lewis Explores Vice and Virtue* (Kansas City: Beacon Hill Press, 2001).
2. Dietrich Bonhoeffer, *The Cost of Discipleship* (New York: Macmillan, 1963).

CHAPTER 8

MAN OF CONTENTMENT

You have just returned home from a great single's retreat where you once again surrendered your frustrations as a single in exchange for God's peace and contentment. As you listen to your answering machine, you hear a certain voice. The most sought-after bachelorette you know is dropping hints about you asking her out on a date. Do you jump at the opportunity to date one of the most eligible girls in town and instantly experience the "Pre-romantic Stress Disorder"? Or do you surrender your expectations dating life to Jesus?

For a single man to experience genuine contentment while soloing in a "couples' world," he must avoid the ditches of discontentment. He needs to learn the mystery of contentment and its power over the restless torture of desire.

The Torture of Desire

It has been said that suffering is having what you do not want (singleness), and wanting what you do not have (a wife). As a single man, you would probably shout "Amen" to such a description of suffering. You know what it is like to get up each day knowing that you do not have what you want—a wife. How do you cope with such a longing?

Longing for what you do not have is a universal condition. It is not limited to singles. It is true that the longing for a wife can be satisfied on your wedding day, but that longing is soon replaced by desires and expectations about the marriage relationship that may not be satisfied in a thousand lifetimes. If you are discontent as a single man, you can count on being dissatisfied as a married man in the future.

The mystery of contentment often seems to escape the understanding of the single man. He assumes that his circumstances justify his condition and give him permission to remain dissatisfied with his life assignment. Not having learned how to lay down the terrible burden of always wanting life to be on his terms, he continues to struggle with the torture of his desires. The restlessness caused by his desire for what he does not have makes waiting seem an impossible task. In fact, to the discontented man, the word *wait* probably compares to a "cuss" word in his mind. The Right Guy finds his capacity to wait for God's best to be rooted in contentment.

Wait

Even after Boaz expressed his willingness to become Ruth's kinsman-redeemer, and Ruth returned home with the good news, Naomi said, "*Wait, my daughter...*" (Ruth 3:18). When God says, "Wait," such an assignment is not to cause suffering, but prevent it. Men experience so much needless pain when they run ahead of God's format. Had Boaz pledged to wed Ruth before he consulted with the nearer kinsman-redeemer, it could have gotten messy. Naomi did not want Ruth's heart to race ahead into disappointment in case the circumstances did not go as assumed.

Ditches of Discontentment

Being single can be difficult enough for a man, but the heartbreak from being "led on" by a woman can dangerously lead to a ditch of discontentment. Some men are so emotionally scarred from falling into such a ditch that it literally takes them years to recover and rediscover the capacity to trust any female in their life. Likewise, some men are unaware of their own capacity to defraud.

"And that no one transgress and defraud his brother in the matter because the Lord is the avenger in all these things..." (1 Thess. 4:6). To defraud is to excite physical or emotional desires that cannot be righteously fulfilled. Since many men do not realize how their actions defraud their sisters in Christ and vice versa, singles need to be aware of such techniques to avoid unnecessary heartbreak and more effectively keep a rein on their emotions.

One way a guy may lead a woman on is by the unwise things he may say or do. A wonderful single guy started a letter one day with the words "Dear Sunshine." When asked who this "Dear Sunshine" was, he said it was his nickname for a girl at college. He came up with this affectionate nickname for her one evening while they stood on a hill overlooking the school as the sun was setting. When asked if they were dating he replied, "Oh, no, we are just friends and there isn't any future for our relationship." He was encouraged to stop calling her Sunshine because it would defraud her emotionally. But, like many men, he had a hard time understanding that calling her Sunshine might cause her to dream about being the "sunshine" in his future after they graduated.

A second way a man might defraud a woman is by ascribing to an unwritten code that has been distributed by Hollywood and swallowed by most of Christianity: friendships with the opposite sex must be romantic and must not establish any emotional boundaries. What Hollywood advocates is like body surfing on the crest of an emotional wave. To establish boundaries seems like an attack on love. Ironically, limits protect real love and leave no room for painful defrauding.

Ken and Jackie established some specific guidelines for their dating relationship in the areas of leadership, communication, and purity. Classmates (even Christians) thought their goals and guidelines would prevent their friendship from blossoming and surviving. Contrary to popular opinion, they have been building on those guidelines for the past 20 years—and romance thrives in their relationship.

In a McDonald's commercial, a guy presents clear guidelines for him and his date. Just before the couple gets to the car, the guy makes one last remark, "I want you to realize that this is just a date, not a commitment and not a proposal." The girl just smiles and continues toward the car, en route to McDonald's and a movie. Now, you may feel his style is just too honest, but such clear communication prevents much misunderstanding between a man's actions and a woman's interpretation of his behavior.

Another way a guy may defraud a woman is by emphasizing the future potential of the relationship rather than focusing on the present opportunities for the friendship to grow. This way of defrauding incites feelings in a woman that cannot be properly fulfilled at that time. This creates emotional turmoil for many women, making it difficult to wait with contentment. Postpone talk of a future together, marriage, or what kind of home you want, until engagement. Do not encourage talk of things that "might be," but rather, encourage words and actions that develop the present friendship.

The Eleventh Commandment

A single man can sabotage his own contentment by defrauding himself as effectively as can his female counterpart. Counselors are constantly helping men and women properly interpret their relationships. Protect your contentment by adopting this "Eleventh Commandment": Thou shalt not defraud thyself.

Men defraud themselves by confusing ministry with matrimony. A guy tries to help a girl grow spiritually, and she sees his care and interest as leading inevitably to marriage. Another guy and girl work on a ministry team together and their spiritual intimacy is confused in her mind with romantic intentions.

Misread intentions between males and females put them on a collision course. The crash can be avoided if the Man of Contentment would keep in mind that his emotions must be submitted to the facts: ministering together is a privilege as a believer, not an automatic marriage opportunity.

To heed the Eleventh Commandment, you must consciously resist doing another good deed for a woman in your life until you know the motive behind your "unselfish" gesture. How many gifts have you already given to some woman in your life because you sensed that the relationship had future dating potential? How many ministries have you participated in because of the chance to be seen by her? How many times have you volunteered to help a sister when you knew you would not be so willing to help a brother in Christ?

The easiest way to break the Eleventh Commandment is to play the surrogate in relation to a sister in Christ. You pick a worthy recipient of your time and attention, then you tend to any special needs you find out about in the guise of unselfish giving. There are single men who fix cars or do house repairs for a girl but haven't even been on their first date with her.

A dedicated Christian should do good deeds, but when you limit your service to the women in your group, it will ultimately backfire. You can end up feeling bruised by your own self-defrauding when you realize the woman has taken your special gestures of service for granted.

Prenuptial Fantasies

An important method of limiting your own self-defrauding is through daily discipline over "prenuptial fantasies." Such fantasies may provide you an escape from monotonous reality, but these moments are dangerous. They will aggravate your struggle for contentment because they are not innocent daydreams, but an attack on your godly contentment. You may be so used to daily fantasies that you might not even realize when you begin daydreaming again about your princess.

Often a single man's struggle with contentment can be traced back to his fantasies more than to his frustrating circumstances. Just think for a moment about three words from Second Corinthians 10:5 (KJV): *"Casting down imaginations."* Fantasizing about a future with a girl you have been watching in Sunday school or at work is nothing more than your very active imagination. What should you do when you start daydreaming about a girl you've never dated or even formally met? You must take your thoughts to Jesus and leave them in His capable hands. This daily discipline of taking your fantasies to Jesus is the foundation for your future as a contented man, whether you are married or single. Right now they are just prenuptial fantasies, but when you are married, those fantasies about other women could continue.

Lack of discipline in the area of "casting down imaginations" may result in self-defrauding and needless discontentment.

Friends too often participate in the development of one's prenuptial fantasies. After only one date with a wonderful woman, a man will share the details of the evening and his friends will not only share his joy, but also foster excessive imaginings by asking questions like, "Do you think this is the one? Should I be planning the bachelor party?" We not only need the discipline of monitoring our own fantasies, but we also need friends who will remind us not to run ahead of God's timing. Such monitoring of our emotions and accountability between friends is so helpful for the Christian single man.

Spiritual Monitor

When a friend excitedly calls to tell you about the evening he has just spent with a special woman, you often know before he gets two paragraphs into his telling of the evening where he is going—fantasy land. As he begins to tell how she is a friend from his past who recently became a Christian and is suddenly back in his life, be careful. It would be easy to say, "Maybe the woman of your dreams is finally here"—but don't. Remember wise Naomi and avoid defrauding your friend. By enthusiastically building false hope in a situation that could be here today but gone before his next paycheck, you can easily help a friend to defraud himself. To help him monitor his reactions, point out that one long-distance phone call from a female friend is not reason enough to take her home to meet his parents. Encourage your friend, instead, to wait until he sees how the friendship develops.

Your monitoring may not be appreciated at first, but the fruit of such counsel will be sweet. This is not to suggest that you cannot share a friend's joy about a wonderful date with a godly woman. But a gift greater than simply sharing his joy is to encourage your friend not to run ahead of the relationship through prenuptial fantasies. Many tears have been shed over relationships that never materialized except in one's dreams.

How can you begin to be a spiritual monitor? The next time a friend is pumped after a date with a wonderful girl, pray for your capacity to share his joy; then pray for the courage to speak the truth about surrendering his dreams to the Lord and not running ahead of Him in his expectations. The spiritual monitor knows the importance of surrendering his own expectations to the only One who can be trusted with his desires and dreams. He can encourage others to surrender their own prenuptial fantasies in exchange for the truth in Psalm 62:5 (KJV): *"My soul, wait thou only upon God; for my expectation is from Him."*

Did you expect to be married by now? Or did you expect to be married forever, and now you are divorced? These expectations mean that you need God's tender loving care and the encouragement of a spiritual monitor who will regularly remind you not to run ahead of the Lord in your relationships with women. Spiritual monitors consistently resist fanning the fire of their friends' enthusiasm. They monitor their responses and limit their reactions to what is reality and not hopeful fantasy.

Ironically, the same close friends who help to accelerate the prenuptial fantasy may be the ones who must comfort the lone lovebird when Miss Right goes out with another guy and no more history is to be made with her. His disappointment will be in direct proportion to the degree that he and his friends responded prematurely to a relationship that will last only in his memory. The next time a friend shares the details of an exciting evening with a beautiful girl, don't overreact. Instead, say to him, "I am thrilled that you had a great time. I am so glad you shared your excitement with me. Now do yourself a favor and before you close your eyes to dream tonight, prayerfully commit Miss Wonderful to Jesus." You will be a true friend and a spiritual monitor for him.

> *Thousands of needless tears,*
> *Produced by careless cheers,*
> *Assuming that Boaz is finally here,*
> *When the arrival of her prince is not*
> *even near...*
> JMK

If you do not have a spiritual monitor in a close friend, then ask the Lord to help you find such a friend.

The Mystery of Contentment

Whether married or single, in prison or at the gym, the key to your enjoying this moment deals with your inner contentment. When your happiness in life is based on "your terms," it is a terrible limitation that will result in a hollow gladness. Singleness does not produce lack of contentment any more than marriage provides contentment. Lack of contentment is the result of the terrible burden of wanting life on your terms.

Married men complain about their lack of contentment as often as single men do, if not more. Both groups of men need to develop the quality of contentment. Paul the apostle, while living in a dark, damp dungeon, wrote of the mystery of contentment that does not depend on circumstances. He described the secret as a "learning process" to which he willingly submitted rather than resisting the conditions.

> Not that I speak from want; for I have learned to be content in **whatever** circumstances I am. I know how to get along with humble means, and I also know how to live in prosperity; in any and every circumstance I have learned the secret of being filled and going hungry, both of having abundance and suffering need. I can do all things through Him who strengthens me (Philippians 4:11-13).

Whether married or single, one must learn that it is Jesus who strengthens you to walk in the most dismal or delightful of circumstances. True contentment is learned. You are not born with it, and you cannot buy it at Lowe's. Your classroom for learning is your daily life. Every shattered dream or unfulfilled expectation serves as a perfect opportunity to learn contentment. These circumstances are your classroom assignments for learning the mystery of contentment. Learning contentment will require complete dependence on Jesus, for difficult circumstances without the strength of Jesus can rob you of potential contentment. Do not be deceived into thinking you do not need Jesus' strength to face the good circumstances as well as the bad. When the sun is shining with no clouds in sight, you may assume that you can securely bask in the sunshine without any prospect of rain; however, this full feeling can easily breed a tendency to ignore Jesus. *"Otherwise, I may have too much and disown you and say, 'Who is the Lord?'"* (Prov. 30:9a NIV).

Stop Arguing With the Umpire

Do you now see the incompatibility of anxiety-filled singleness and contented godliness?

Are you ready to rid yourself of the ditches of discontentment that have robbed you of so much peace and joy?

Defrauding by a woman, a friend, or even oneself will aggravate your lack of contentment; however, the source of your lack is not defrauding or even frustrating circumstances. Your lack of contentment is because of *pride*. Pride can be described as an excessively high opinion of what one deserves. When a single's life is not moving in the direction he wants (wife, career, children, house, etc.) the arguing often begins. With whom is the single man arguing? It is none other than the umpire, the arbitrator: Jesus. *"Let the peace of Christ rule* [arbitrate, umpire] *in your hearts..."* (Col. 3:15).

The struggle with the Umpire is not limited to the single men up to bat! Every man must learn to trust the call of his heavenly Umpire. The trouble from the beginning was a man and woman not listening to the Umpire, but reaching out for a life on "their terms." "I was safe!" you yell. The Umpire says, "No, you were out!" Why would people argue with such an all-wise Umpire? *"Pride only breeds quarrels"* (Prov. 13:10a).

Consider a very poignant verse that brilliantly reveals the war in all of us. *"What causes fights and quarrels among you? Don't they come from your desires that battle within you?* **You want something but don't get it...***"* (James 4:1-2 NIV). Honestly face any struggle you may have with your pride-driven desire to have life on your terms. Exchange your pride for Jesus' strength so you may accept whatever calls the Umpire makes from this moment forward. Dating is not a reward or a prize for living for Jesus.

Argue too much with God and you might be removed from the game—for your own benefit. A Friday night without a date is often a night of "being sent to the showers" by an all-wise Umpire. *My soul finds rest in God alone...* (Ps. 62:1).

Becoming a Man of Contentment

Do you have a spiritual monitor? If not, what can you do about finding the right one? Perhaps you have a friend you want to help as a spiritual monitor. Are you intimidated by the prospect of this role in his life? Why? Read Proverbs 28:23

and Hebrews 3:13. If you are a spiritual monitor, how can you become more effective?

_____

_____

_____

A contented man has the ability to lay down the terrible burden of always needing life on his terms. Are you a contented man? Take the time to read and ponder Matthew 11:28-30, Hebrews 13:5, Philippians 4:11, Judges 21:25, Luke 1:38, and Matthew 26:39. As a follower of Jesus, what can you do to become contented?

_____

_____

_____

Pride is an excessively high opinion of what one deserves. Do you struggle with pride's control of your desires? Read Proverbs 13:10, 16:18, 29:23; Jeremiah 5:3; and James 4:1-2.

_____

_____

_____

Does toe-tapping, nail-biting, "I'm a quarter past 30 years old" thinking rob you of contentment? What limits God from acting on your behalf? Read Matthew 6:27, Isaiah 30:18, and 64:4.

_____

_____

_____

_____

_____

_____

_____

_____

_____

_____

_____

_____

_____

_____

_____

_____

CHAPTER 9

MAN OF CONVICTION

D oes it seem too unrealistic for today's man to set his sights on a princess? Is it only the rare idealist who gets lucky and finds a woman who satisfies his list of 30 traits? A single friend (a modern Ruth) wrote a letter in which she admitted that her high ideals often made her feel like the "Lone Ranger." She said, "So often, I meet men who don't want to go the deeper, more radical route of separation from our culture in seeking after God's standards." Do we lower our standards because we seem out of step with all our peers? Does the woman in Proverbs 31 seem obsolete? Maybe for the worldly man she is obsolete, but not for the Man of Conviction. God has the best in hand for those who seek Him.

Isaac submitted to his father Abraham and Abraham's trusted servant to select his bride—a prayer-bathed journey that is a type and a shadow of the Holy Spirit calling out the Bride for the Son. Likewise, Boaz did not marry until God brought Ruth to him—and his son, Obed, became part of the lineage of Jesus Christ,

After becoming a Christian, Jackie found herself ashamed of her lack of a proper upbringing. She says this:

> I knew I had been forgiven for the past, but I often wrestled with the feelings of being damaged goods. I found myself envying other girls who were from godly homes and great heritages, spiritually. Whenever I would be introduced to a wonderful Christian guy, I would immediately think, *I'm not good enough.*

> This was exactly how I felt when I first met my husband. He had asked Jesus to take control of his life at the young age of 11. He went to church faithfully; he never smoked, drank, or fooled around sexually. His high standards were very intimidating to me. Throughout the years of our friendship, I knew he would never

date me because of my imperfect past and ungodly family. Was I in for a surprise! As I continued to make choices to break the ungodly influences of my past, the Lord was working on bringing Ken and me together as a team for His glory. Like David I thought, *"Who am I, O Sovereign Lord, and what is my family, that you have brought me this far?"* (2 Sam. 7:18b NIV).

Ungodly cycles can be broken. Your destiny is not something that is left to chance or fate; it is the product of wise choices.

Destiny—Chance or Choice?

Do you think your ideals and standards are too high? Do you feel the pressure to compromise and settle for the generic version of life? Ruth lived in an era that was exactly like modern America. Judges 21:25 describes the era in which she lived: *"In those days there was no king in Israel; everyone did what was right in his own eyes."* We too live in a culture where it seems that no one fears God and people just "do their own thing."

You, like Ruth, will be greatly affected by your choices. Ruth's wise choices allowed her to break a godless family cycle and begin a new cycle that the Word of God triumphantly records. God has not changed—and neither have women. The high standards in God's Word are not irrelevant, but completely applicable to finding God's best for your life. Choices, guided by your convictions rather than by chance, determine your destiny. How wise have your decisions been in the past in regard to relating to and dating women? Have you made some poor choices that you can see were the result of your own lack of proper convictions in the areas of love, sex, and dating? Your present choices will affect the rest of your life in this delicate area that is often a collision course—male/female relating.

You cannot make good choices without proper, biblical convictions. Don't carelessly leave your dating/relating standards to chance. Too much depends on your decisions in this area. A stanza from the song "Guard Your Heart" by Jon Mohr captures this warning:

The human heart is easily swayed
And often betrayed
At the hand of emotion.
We dare not leave the outcome to
chance;
We must choose in advance
Or live in agony
Such needless tragedy.[1]

From the beginning of time, God has shown His own people exactly what course they should take to avoid needless tragedy. A passage of Scripture that clearly states the reality of our own choices of happiness or misery is Deuteronomy 30:15-20. Remember that the media, music, literature, teachers, and peers often oppose the godly choices that you might want to make.

Standard-Bearer

May we go back to the basics for just a moment? What is a conviction, and how does one develop biblical convictions? A conviction is a standard that serves as a springboard for your choices. Consider where your standards, in the area of relating and dating, originated. Are your standards based more on Hollywood's terms of love and romance, or have you allowed God's holy Word to shape your perspective?

The Man of Conviction gives the Lord permission to renew his mind on a daily basis. He spends time searching the Word of God for standards that will guide him safely to God's best. He has made a significant choice as a godly man. He has surrendered his mind to a new persuasion: God's perspective on love and romance. The convictions that he establishes, based on the Word, allow him to resist being squeezed into the mold of this world. He is a nonconformist in a biblical sense, as in Romans 12:2 NIV, which says, *"Do not conform any longer to the pattern of this world, but be transformed by the renewing of your mind. Then you will be able to test and approve what God's will is—His good, pleasing and perfect will."* Notice the words test and approve; your convictions (whether Hollywood-based or Bible-based) gauge your ability to "test and approve" the relationships you've had or will have.

If you want to live by God's standards for love, sex, and dating, you must prepare yourself for the inevitable resistance that "standard-bearers" face. When you live by your convictions, many of your friends will consider you unrealistic. Some of your friends may even think you are stubbornly opinionated. Facing such opposition from the people you love is not easy, but the Lord will give you the grace to refuse to compromise. A true standard-bearer wants to be a vanguard in a movement. Through Jesus' strength, you can stand firm, unwavering, as you wait for His best. The man without the high ideals that the Word of God sets forth leaves his choices to chance. He will tend to end up with a Bimbo rather than a Ruth because he cannot measure accurately the woman behind the "makeup."

Since most biblical convictions are in opposition to all the propaganda from Hollywood, relatively few, even among Christians, hold to these standards. This harsh reality is revealed throughout the Word. James 4:4-5 (Phillips) says:

> *You are like unfaithful wives, never realizing that to be the world's lover means becoming the enemy of God! Anyone who chooses to be the world's friend is thereby making himself God's enemy. Or do you think what the scriptures have to say about this is a mere formality?*

When you pass up dates with certain girls because you know they do not measure up to God's standards, then you have taken seriously your commitment not to oppose God. If your friends pressure and oppose you, ask the Lord for the strength to be more concerned with being His friend and not His enemy through compromising standards.

In America, government agencies regulate the standards of the food that you consume on a daily basis. For example, meat is subject to federal regulation of its grade, weight, and quality. How much more significant than ground beef (even prime rib) is the woman with whom you hope to share the rest of your life? Such consideration and evaluation cannot be obtained through a glance or chance encounter at the "meet" counter. A lifelong relationship demands the highest standards of regulation. There are women breathing on this planet today who can handle such scrutiny and be found "worth waiting for."

Avoiding Bimbos

What is a Bimbo? A Bimbo is a girl whose outward appearance is a façade. It is hard to discern who she really is because of the "makeup and costume" she wears. What she appears to be physically, socially, and even spiritually is just a performance. A Bimbo is a counterfeit of a Ruth.

It is possible to avoid such a clown. Your standards and convictions will help you recognize the difference. The remainder of this chapter will accentuate the genuine Ruth. Concentrating on the real thing will make the Bimbos more apparent.

Before any guy asks a girl out on the first date, he should have established in his heart and mind a biblical alternative to Hollywood's dating style. As a prerequisite to every date, you should examine your motive (elaborated in the chapter on contentment). Are you going out with this girl because you haven't had a date in years? Are you going out with someone who may not really be a Christian because you think a date—even with a Bimbo—is better than no date at all? Many men spend time with girls who do not really care for them. They would rather waste an evening with a Bimbo than face another lonely night in a dateless condition. Some men even give up their biblical convictions in order to get a date with a certain girl. Do you feel as though you allow your dating schedule to determine your personal worth? Many single men are prisoners of the world's dating syndrome. They equate their self-worth with how many dates they had last month.

Have you dated more Bimbos than Ruths? If your answer is yes, you may need to develop higher ideals.

One Auburn University graduate left school with not only a diploma, but also a very specific list of the qualities she was looking for in a future mate. See if her list (with the genders switched) contains any of the qualities you are looking for in Miss Right:

- Spirit-controlled Christian (see Eph. 5:18).

- Jesus is #1 in her life, not just an ornament (see Mark 12:30).

- Broken; understands how to rely totally upon Jesus (see Phil. 4:13).

- Ministry-minded; wherever she is, she is available (see 1 Cor. 4:2).

- Motivator; woman of vision, concerned about lost souls (see Rom. 10:14).

- Sensitive spirit; in tune to the needs of others (see Gal. 6:2).

- Understands the awesome responsibility of a wife to her husband (see Eph. 5:25-31).

- Humble enough to be a disciple (teachable) and able to disciple others (see Matt. 28:19-20).

- Woman of prayer; she knows the key to success is her private time with God (see Col. 4:2).

- Family woman; she desires to have children and raise them properly for God's glory (see Prov. 22:6).

Clear standards for dating and relating will guard you against compromise and making wrong choices out of sudden emotion rather than a God-directed will. These guidelines for your dating friendships will keep God as your focus rather than allowing the girl to become the focus (idol). Clear standards coupled with accountability to a brother in Christ will help you walk in the convictions you establish. To guard you against haphazard meetings or just the "WFs" (weird feelings) in your heart, you need standards for which you will be accountable.

A disclaimer that we would like to include at this point is not to simplify the reason so many men are attracted to Bimbos. The issue of standards is most relevant, but may seem simplistic. We acknowledge that some men find it difficult to raise their standards and change their patterns because they are still entangled with the past. Unresolved conflicts with a mother, a sister, or an ex-girlfriend may overshadow and control the attraction to Bimbos. In this case, we suggest a possible date fast, a period of time during which you refrain from accepting another date until you can sort out some of the unresolved conflicts from the past. This method has been used by many single men who have been entangled with old dating patterns. During the "date fast," they find time to search for new ways of relating and dating biblically.

If you have already spent time with the Lord establishing dating/relating standards, then you will receive affirmation through the following material. If you have been letting your dating routine be controlled by chance rather than biblical choice, consider not accepting another date until you have nailed down your convictions. Too much is at stake.

Once you have set dating standards and understand the significance of a constant motive check, (daily bringing the thoughts and intentions of your heart to the Lord), you are ready to consider other guidelines for successful dating and relating.

The author's son, Ben, says that you can sidestep a lifetime of unhappiness by merely being aware of these deal breakers in a potential date:

1. Speaking *Christianese,* rather than having a growing relationship with Jesus

2. Nonnegotiable flaws—addiction and abuse (verbal or physical)

3. Personality quirks that you can't live with for a lifetime

Wedding Day Chains

If a man chooses to walk down the aisle with an unbeliever, he faces a future in chains—not because he married a female member of a motorcycle gang—but because he made an unwise choice. The Word of God speaks clearly about a partnership with an unbeliever. A common verse used for this conviction is Second Corinthians 6:14-17, but you find a more poignant message for the one who wavers in this conviction in Joshua.

> *But if you turn away and ally your-selves with the survivors of these na-tions that remain among you and if you intermarry with them and associ-ate with them, then you may be sure that the Lord your God will no longer drive out these nations before you. In-stead, they will become snares and traps for you, whips on your backs and thorns in your eyes, until you perish from this good land, which the Lord your God has given you* (Joshua 23:12-13 NIV).

One would be foolish to disobey God in the area of marrying an unbeliever.

When a single man experiences a prolonged period of datelessness, loneliness tempts him to compromise his conviction concerning dating a growing Christian. His dateless state may pres-sure him to surrender to the temptation of dat-ing an unbeliever. He may justify such a date in the guise of being a witness for Jesus. Many single men have been trapped emotionally with an unbeliever when it all began with "missionary dating." Ponder this: Every unbelieving marriage partner arrived as an unbeliever on the first date. As trite as it may seem, every date is a potential mate. Avoid dating an unbeliever.

Many men want so desperately to date that the only qualification they have for the girl is that she goes to church. Every Sunday churches have people attending to appease God or to satisfy a religious urge. You must set a higher standard and resist dating a girl who is not growing in her intimacy with Christ.

The Woman-Worth-Waiting-For

How would you describe the ideal woman, a "Woman-Worth-Waiting-For?" Too many girls want to talk about Jesus for 60 seconds and their friends or job or latest trip to the mall for the rest of the evening. Are there women who agree with Psalm 73:25: *"Whom have I in heaven but You* [the Lord]? *And besides You, I desire nothing on earth."* Do such spiritual women exist? Yes, but they are exceptions and not the rule. Their appearance requires waiting on the part of the recipient.

Before considering the specific qualities found in a Ruth, one should deal with certain physical stereotypes. Whether you have been looking for a bronzed, blue-eyed blonde (BBB) or a pert, petite brunette (PBB), you need to surrender your desires to the Lord. Everyone has certain preferences. But such a mind-set needs to be given to Jesus. Too many single men have missed wonderful treasures in godly girls because the treasure was not encased in a BBB or PBB. The Lord will probably not require you to date a girl who repulses you physically. But you need to be open to girls who do not fit your desired stereotype. Too often a girl may satisfy your eyesight but leave your heart empty and still longing. Remember, after a few years that bronzed, blue-eyed blonde can be transformed into a pale, wrinkly girl with bifocals on those gorgeous eyes.

How many men, after the honeymoon is over, feel like they married a stranger? How many newlyweds are disillusioned by their mate's behavior within a few months of marriage? Most marriage counseling problems have their roots in personality problems—not physiques.

The Book of Ruth tells the story of an ideal wife. You want to marry someone for the qualities she possesses now, not for the qualities you hope she will develop. The most common mistake made by marriage partners is marrying someone they intend to change. Since it is nearly impossible to change a person, you will want to set standards of dating or of building friendships with women who are characterized by the following qualities. A single man can sidestep a lifetime of tragedy by seriously considering these characteristics in a prospective steady date:

- Puts the needs of others ahead of her own. This woman accepts people just the way they are, loving others even when her love is not returned. She will continue to love someone because of her commitment to that person, not because of how she feels.

  Do nothing from selfishness or empty conceit, but with humility of mind regard one another as more important than yourselves; do not merely look out for your own personal interests, but also for the interests of others (Philippians 2:3-4).

- Rejoices in her relationship with Christ. You don't have to ask this woman if she is a Christian. Her joy in the Lord is evident in her life.

These things I have spoken to you, so that My joy may be in you, and that your joy may be made full (John 15:11).

- Maintains proper relationships. This woman seeks a good relationship with everyone—from her friends to her parents. She listens to differing perspectives without feeling threatened. She has the strength to back off from a fight. She works to forgive wrongs done to her and seeks to make her own offenses right. She will not hold a grudge.

Pursue peace with all men... (Hebrews 12:14).

- Refuses to jump ahead of God's timing. She is not so eager to be something, do something, or have something that she cannot wait on God's timing. She chooses against impulsiveness so she may be in the exact center of God's will.

Rest in the Lord and wait patiently for Him... (Psalm 37:7).

- Seeks to meet the practical needs of others. She is not so self-absorbed that she cannot make time for the needy. She is interested in the welfare of others and is willing to give her time, money, and energy for their benefit.

Be kind to one another, tender-hearted... (Ephesians 4:32).

• Stands for what is right. She hates anything contrary to God's holy character. She is known as a woman of integrity by those with whom she works.

There will be...glory and honor and peace to everyone who does good... (Romans 2:9-10).

• Follows through on her God-given responsibilities. She uses the talents God has given her and realizes that "she + Jesus = adequacy for any God-given job." She is neither overconfident nor absorbed with feelings of inferiority. She is not a dreamer, wishing for more ability, but a diligent steward of the talents she has been given. This woman is dependable and stays with even a difficult task until it is completed.

Now it is required that those who have been given a trust must prove faithful (1 Corinthians 4:2).

- Understands the importance of feelings and emotions. Some men may find themselves attracted to a demanding woman, assuming that her dominance will be their security. Other men may marry a doormat they can dominate, but inevitably end up despising the woman's weakness. A gentle woman is the best of both; she takes the initiative to lead but tempers it with gentle responses toward the other's feelings.

So, as those who have been chosen of God, holy and beloved, put on a heart of compassion, kindness, humility, gentleness and patience (Colossians 3:12).

- Flees temptations to compromise. This woman refuses to be in situations that are sensual, immoral, or impure. She does not entertain friendships that lead to drunkenness or carousing. She avoids talk that could cause strife or jealousy. This woman does not allow a temper to control her or anger to destroy her.

Like a city that is broken into and without walls is a man who has no control over his spirit (Proverbs 25:28).

These qualities are not unrealistic ideals. When a woman follows Jesus, the Holy Spirit works these into her life. In fact, you can read this list again and match the fruit of the Spirit with the appropriate characteristic. *"But the fruit of the Spirit is love, joy, peace, patience, kindness, goodness, faithfulness, gentleness, self-control; against such things there is no law"* (Gal. 5:22-23).

None of the women you date will have all these qualities perfected. All of us are at differing levels of maturity. A woman of God is one who works toward being conformed to the character of Christ. But be careful when a quality of God's Spirit is completely missing in a woman's life and she is unwilling to deal with it before marriage. Realize that if character is absent before the wedding ceremony, it will be missing after the wedding ceremony and cause considerable problems during marriage.

Was Ruth Boaz's Woman-Worth-Waiting-For, the last person of godly character, or was she just one of many? We are convinced that God still grooms Ruths for His sons today. This does not mean a girl has to be perfect in order for you to go out with her. It does mean that she needs to be growing in Christlikeness by the enabling power of the Holy Spirit before you start to date her.

Do you want to marry a princess? Then set your standards high. To be married to a woman who loves the Lord and wants to serve Him is one of life's highest privileges. It is worth whatever wait, whatever cost. Nail down your convictions and refuse to compromise by dating women who are not controlled by God's Holy Spirit. These standards will stand guard over the castle of your heart. Proverbs 4:23 NIV says, *"**Above all else, guard your heart**, for it is the wellspring of life."*

Becoming a Man of Conviction

Write out your standards for the kind of girls you will date and the Scriptures where you found those qualities. What convictions led you to select these particular standards?

_____

_____

_____

_____

_____

What is the problem with dating girls who are good, but who are not Christians? What is the difference between a good woman who goes to church and a growing Christian woman? What difference would it make in marriage?

_____

_____

If the wait becomes hard and you meet someone who loves you, but has a glaring character flaw, what will you sacrifice if you marry her? Look through each of the characteristics found in the Woman-Worth-Waiting-For section and determine what could be lost in your marriage if that quality was missing in your wife and the mother of your children.

_____

_____

Put a check beside each of the following characteristics that *you* can change in your wife after marriage:

___ Unwillingness to communicate (see Prov. 14:10)

___ Dominating ego (see Rom. 12:3)

___ Bad temper (see James 1:19-20)

___ Argumentative tendencies (see Prov. 20:3)

___ Difficulty in apologizing (see Eph. 4:32)

___ Bad language (see Eph. 5:4)

___ Unwillingness to be involved with church (see Heb. 10:24-25

___ Inability to keep a job (see 1 Tim. 5:8)

___ Jealousy (see 1 Cor. 13:4)

___ Self-centeredness (see 2 Cor. 5:15)

___ Depression (see 2 Cor. 4:16)

___ Unwillingness to give (see 2 Cor. 9:7)

___ Hanging out with worldly friends (see 1 Cor. 15:33

___ Flirtatious (see 1 Thess. 4:2-7)

___ Lying (see Eph. 4:25)

___ Immaturity (see Eph. 4:15)

___ Covetous (see 1 Tim. 6:7-11)

What does the Bible say about these qualities in reference to godliness? What will you most likely face in your marriage and family life if your wife does not have an intimate relationship with Jesus Christ (see 2 Cor. 3:18)?

Endnote

1. Jon Mohr, "Guard Your Heart," copyright 1989 Birdwing Music.

CHAPTER **10**

MAN OF PATIENCE

W hile the Book of Ruth portrays Boaz as a man of integrity who honors God, it does not offer many details of his life as a young man. One thing we do know is that he was older than the workers in his field with whom Ruth was acquainted (see Ruth 3:10). One has to wonder how an older man can be patient when there appears to be no end to the waiting in sight. Waiting isn't easy when you are young, and it can be terribly hard as you get older.

God demonstrated His faithfulness in a special way to Ruth and Boaz, who chose to wait for His best, whether they married or not. They witnessed God's faithfulness in marriage and children as in singleness because they waited on His perfect timing for their future.

Take courage, single friend. You are not alone in your wait; neither are you alone in the feelings and struggles you encounter. Many godly men have waited and won. Many men have lost hope and compromised. Wait patiently and win triumphantly the future your Father has planned for you. It will always be designed with you in mind and is worth being patient to discover.

Though we do not know what Boaz went through as he waited for a wife, he is an example of a person of patience. In Ruth 4:13, we see the end to their love story. *"So Boaz took Ruth, and she became his wife...."*

Why Is Waiting So Hard?

If God is faithful, why is it so easy to lose patience? Why is it so hard to wait? Why is it easier to settle for less than God's best? Fear is a huge hindrance to waiting. You may fear that your biological clock is ticking away and God has not noticed. You may fear, with every wedding you attend, that soon you will no longer have any single friends. You might feel that you better marry this "OK girl" who seems to like you a lot because she's pretty good and you fear you may not find another. Or possibly you fear loneliness and a lifetime of eating by yourself and of going to a church filled with people, only to sit alone.

Fear is an internal pressure. There are external pressures as well. Society pushes single men to marry before they are too "old." Friends play matchmaker, your parents want grandchildren, and your cousins want to know, "What's wrong with you?" You feel like you don't fit in with the youth any longer, but you can't very well go to the young married couples' functions at church (where your friends now attend). The world is attacking a single man's confidence as the enemy discourages his hopes through fear. These pressures often provoke single men to take more initiative rather than patiently wait for God's best.

Consequences of Impatience

There are grave consequences for the single man who does not choose to develop patience and wait on God's timing. Society is full of heartbreaking examples. Some end in divorce; others end in an emotional separation that causes the husband and wife to merely live under the same roof. Some leave precious children damaged by the insecurity and fear that an unhealthy marriage produces. The personal loneliness and hurt that these lifestyles bring is an anguish that is indescribable. God did not intend a man to have to live like that.

Impatience to find a woman can cause a man to argue about his "right" to date a woman who is not godly, maybe not even a Christian. In Joshua 23:12-14 the Lord warns His people not to marry unbelievers. God knows that an ungodly wife will end up being *"snares and traps for you, whips on your backs and thorns in your eyes..."* (Josh. 23:13 NIV). Many young men argue that they are just dating, not marrying an unbeliever. But think about this—in our society, does anyone ever marry someone he or she never dated? Every date is a potential mate.

Marriage to a non-Christian brings pain to the believing husband. As a man, you long to be known and loved for all you are. A woman who is spiritually dead can never know the very intimate spiritual part of you that is your heart. She would be blind to much of what you would try to share with her. She could never know and understand you fully.

Be careful when you begin to think that you are "in love" and you "just can't live without her." Think again. Think of the loneliness you will feel when your wife will not attend church with you. Think of the angry bickering that may take place between the two of you because she can never understand the depths of your spiritual awareness and, consequently, your convictions. If you do not think about this now, you may one day think, "Before, I couldn't live without her; now I can hardly live with her." Second Corinthians 6:14-15 is very clear: *"Do not be bound together with unbelievers; for what partnership have righteousness and lawlessness, or what fellowship has light with darkness? Or what harmony has Christ with Belial, or what has a believer in common with an unbeliever?"*

Please consider a greater consequence than being unhappily married to a woman who does not know your Lord. Will you be able to handle the pain of watching your children live with possible rejection by their mother, day in and day out? Will you think it is worth the cost when you are the only one who gets up on Sunday mornings to take your children to church? Will it be worth the compromise when your children look up at you and ask why mommy doesn't love Jesus? They could even reject the Lord for eternity and live a miserable, ill-chosen lifestyle because of the choice you made to marry a wonderful, but lost, woman. Children will often follow their father's example—good or bad. Exodus 34:7 gives a warning you cannot ignore: "...*He will by no means leave the guilty unpunished, visiting the iniquity of fathers on the children and on the grandchildren to the third and fourth generations.*" You are not just marrying a wife, but choosing a mother for your children.

When you marry, you do not choose blessings or curses for you alone; you choose for the generations after you. If you choose to wait patiently for your princess, you will be blessed by the heritage that a princess brings. If you choose to run eagerly ahead of God's plan and marry a woman with no conscience toward God, you will reap the life's course she follows, but not alone. Your children's and grandchildren's lives will be directly affected by the woman you marry.

Consider the following Scriptures:

> *All these blessings will come upon you and overtake you if you will obey the Lord your God* (Deuteronomy 28:2).

> *But it shall come about, if you do not*
> *obey the Lord your God...all these*
> *curses shall come upon you and*
> *overtake you* (Deuteronomy 28:15).

God warned His people in Deuteronomy of the long-term effect of their choices. Today other countries may not take our children, but there are many bondages in our wicked generation that could hold them.

> *Your sons and your daughters shall*
> *be given to another people, while your*
> *eyes look on and yearn for them con-*
> *tinually; but there will be nothing you*
> *can do* (Deuteronomy 28:32).

Have you seen the eyes of a father as he sees his son on drugs or his daughter living on the streets? There is nothing he can do but look on in pain.

Deuteronomy 28:2, 15, and 32 show that God has always desired to bless His people, but He will not force them to do what is best. In His Word He has often warned us to wait, to be careful, and to trust Him. He will not make us wait. His heart of love begs us to listen and obey so He may bless us and the dear ones who will one day look to and follow us. The words He gave to the children of Israel in Deuteronomy 30:15-20 show the love and concern He has for the choices you make.

> *...So choose life in order that you may live, you and your descendants, by loving the Lord your God, by obeying His voice, and by holding fast to Him...* (Deuteronomy 30:19-20).

You must choose to wait patiently for God's best. If you have seen patterns in your life that show a lack of patience, commit yourself right now to waiting for God's best.

You may pray something like this:

> Lord, You are my sovereign God. You know all about me and love me more than anyone else ever could. You know how I feel, what I need, and what my future is. I confess that I have taken matters into my own hands. I confess to being afraid of totally trusting You. Today I commit myself to focus on You and Your

love for me. Today I commit to look to You for my future—not to my outward circumstances. Thank You for knowing how weak I feel, but being strong for me and in me. I love You. I choose to trust You.

You may have to repeat this prayer, or one like it, many times when you feel afraid. But Psalm 103:13-14 assures us that He understands and has compassion on us:

> *Just as a father has compassion on his children, so the Lord has compassion on those who fear Him. For He Himself knows our frame; He is mindful that we are but dust* (Psalm 103:13-14).

Developing Patience

Wait patiently. Perhaps you are giving God time to prepare, not yourself, but your beloved. Let your heavenly Father accomplish His work thoroughly while your single woman is undistracted. Issues settled in a person's life while single limit unnecessary stress and difficulty later in a marriage. Psalm 37:7 says, *"Rest in the Lord and wait patiently for Him...."* Wait not for a woman or a preconceived perfect future, but for Him. Verses 3, 4, and 5 of Psalm 37 give some great action words for the Man of Patience to follow in order to wait before Him.

Realizing that marriage is not a dream but real life can also help you to wait more patiently. Instead of merely being envious, get with a godly married man and see the extra load he carries. Look at all he cannot do, instead of the fact that he has a woman in his house. Understand that in reality, married life is not constant communication, daily roses, hugs and kisses, breakfast in bed, and sheer bliss. Marriage is every bit as much work as it is wonderful, even in God's way and time. It is good, but don't be deceived into mistaking it for Heaven.

Since no spouse is perfect, learning to live "as one" is not without its tears. Marriage alone is not a cure-all or answer to every heartfelt need. If you think it is, you had better just keep waiting, for that kind of marriage doesn't exist. Although there is a romantic inside every one of us, you must be realistic regarding marriage or the shock could be devastating.

Find other single guys and plan activities. Don't just sit at home on Friday night. Go out to eat, or to the movies, and become involved working with children, young people, or senior adults. There are many things you can do to stay busy and keep from becoming impatient.

Developing patience is hard. Getting married ahead of God's timing is worse. God may not work according to your time schedule, but He does have your best interests in mind.

You don't know what tomorrow holds, but you do know who holds tomorrow. Say this with the psalmist:

> *O Lord, my heart is not proud, nor my eyes haughty; nor do I involve myself in great matters, or in things too difficult for me. Surely I have composed and quieted my soul; like a weaned child rests against his mother, my soul is like a weaned child within me. O* [substitute your name], *hope in the Lord from this time forth and forever* (Psalm 131).

The place of rest that the psalmist found was a result of the choice he made. This quietness of soul did not come naturally to him. He actively chose to take himself out of involvement and quiet his soul (his mind, will, and emotions). He chose to put his hope in God. Are you trying to involve yourself in matters that are too great for you? Can you see into a woman's heart? Can you know the future? You know Someone who does know women's hearts and the future. Patiently rest in Him. He will bring you the peace you need. This attitude of patience is not something that will just happen. By an act of your will you must choose to trust God regardless of what happens. Patiently wait for His best.

Every single man must at some point come to grips with the fact that not all men will marry. Marriage is not a need, though God chooses to let marriage meet some needs a man may have. Marriage is not a right, though God chooses to plan marriage for the majority of men. Marriage does not complete a person, though men who properly marry find that marriage rounds out some of their weaknesses. If marriage were a need, right, or completion for men, then all godly men would marry. There are many examples of true, God-honoring men who had no earthly mate but were still Men of Patience.

Read the following two testimonies of single women from this perspective: Regardless of whether you are male or female, you are a member of the Body of Christ, the church who is His Bride.

One Lady in Waiting wrote this:

> I believe part of being a Lady of Patience is honestly facing the future. For me that was realizing that I might not ever get married.
>
> I could handle the thoughts of 'waiting on the Lord,' but to face the reality that it may not be His desire for me to marry was hard to cope with. As I read my Bible, I found Isaiah 54:5. The verse said I was already married to Him. He was my Husband! I was His bride. He wanted me to know Him, my Husband. He wanted me to see myself as His bride, to know His love for me. He wanted to be intimate with me. So I began my walk with my Husband, the Lord Jesus.
>
> I still desire to get married; in fact, many times I have longed for

a husband and even cried for one. There have been times when I thought I had met 'the one for me,' then was terribly disappointed. But I always knew I could go back to my 'Husband' who understood my desire and my hurts. He would encourage me by showing me His love in even deeper ways.

Another single woman named Beverly developed the following Bible study to calm the impatience of her heart.

By Beverly Seward Brandon

Why Do I Want to Get Married?	How Can God Meet Those Needs in My Life?
I want to be loved.	"...*I have loved you with an everlasting love...*" (Jer. 31:3).
I want someone to adore me.	The King has brought me into his chambers to adore me. My lover is outstanding among 10,000 (see Song 1:4; 5:10).

Why Do I Want to Get Married?	How Can God Meet Those Needs in My Life?
I want someone to hold *my hand.*	*"...I will uphold you with My righteous right hand"* (Is. 41:10).
I want to be accepted and valued.	I am accepted in the Beloved (see Eph. 1:6 KJV).
I want a "place," a nesting place that is my own to create and use.	We can rest in the shadow of the Almighty (see Ps. 91:1).
I want help in my days *of trouble.*	*"Call upon Me in the day of trouble; I shall rescue you..."* (Ps. 50:15).
I want to share my life—the joys and the struggles—with one person (intimacy)	God will share with me the treasures of darkness and hidden riches (see Is. 45:3).
I want a champion of *my causes— one who* is willing to fight for me.	*"The Lord will fight for you..."* (Ex. 14:14).

Why Do I Want to Get Married?	How Can God Meet Those Needs in My Life?
I want someone to meet my needs.	God is meeting all my needs (see Phil. 4:19).
I want intimacy.	The Lord is intimate with the upright (see Ps. 140:13).
I want someone to help me in my life.	There is no one like God who rides the heavens to help you (see Deut. 33:26).
I want to walk through life sustained and carried. I don't want the whole load of life.	Even to my old age, God will sustain me, carry me, and rescue me (see Is. 46:4).
I want a companion for this life.	God invites us to humbly walk with Him (see Mic. 6:8).
I desire children.	God gives us spiritual children like the numberless grains of sand if we invest in lives (see Is. 48:19).

Beverly's response to this study is: "The Lord, my Maker, is my Husband. Only He can meet the deepest needs of my heart. No man can ever come through for me fully. Only He can. He is what I long for. Only God is enough."

Regardless of what you see or what you feel, God is in full control of your situation. You, Right Guy, can walk in victory by choosing to be patient in your wait.

Don't let your impatient longings rob you of the life God wants to bless you with as a single. Realize you do not need marriage for happiness or a full life. If you are holding onto marriage as a right, relinquish this right so it will not keep you from God's fullest blessings. God knows what is best for you. His timing is perfect, and He will take care of His Man of Patience.

Why the Right Guy May Need to Be Patient With the Right Girl

When it comes to God's best for a woman, it involves so much more than just a great guy. A man worth waiting for is a man who can handle "her particular baggage." For example, my Boaz had to handle the "baggage" I brought with me on our honeymoon. That baggage contained the impact of a most dysfunctional family and sexual abuse. Such heavy "baggage" would not have been handled as graciously by just any man—God knew the man that would have enough faith to patiently love me as Jesus and I sorted through so much baggage.

Boaz was a symbol of Jesus as our Kinsman-Redeemer, who bought us back from the enemy of our soul. Jesus, like a Boaz, can handle the baggage of our life and He can pick the man that can handle such "baggage" without moving into bitterness or resentment.

How interesting that the leading man, Mr. Darcy, in the movie/book *Pride and Prejudice,* had to handle with integrity and grace some family baggage and financial needs—baggage that was present in the life of his love—even prior to marriage. But this baggage did not deter him from caring and pursuing the woman he loved.

Becoming a Man of Patience

Write out the things that make you lose patience. Which of these cause your Sovereign God concern?

Give these concerns to Him and ask Him to help you trust while you wait. "I will trust while I wait, for my God is never late" is a good motto.

_____

_____

_____

Read Deuteronomy 28:1-48. Write on one side of a piece of paper the blessings God wanted the nation of Israel to have as His children. Write on the other side what He asked them to do. What does He require of you? Confess any ways that you have disobeyed God's will for your life and ask Him to help you obey with faith and patience.

_____

_____

_____

Use an exhaustive concordance of the Bible to study the word "patience." (Keep in mind that "patience" in the NIV is translated "longsuffering" or "endurance" in some Bible versions.) Write five blessings that result when a believer practices patience. What is the source of patience for the believer in First Timothy 1:16, Galatians 5:22, and

Colossians 1:11? In Hebrews 6:12, what spiritual quality works together with patience as you wait for God's blessings and will to be revealed?

_____

_____

_____

Make Psalm 27 or Isaiah 40:31 your prayer and commit it, or another passage, to memory to use on those hard days.

_____

_____

_____

_____

_____

_____

_____

_____

_____

_____

More Information about our authors:

Jackie Kendall

Power to Grow Ministries

www.jackiekendall.com

Debby Jones

Crossover Communications International

P.O. Box 211755
Columbia, SC 29221
1.803.691.0688